STEAM at SWIN

The R C 'Dick' Riley Archive: Vol 5
Compiled by Andrew Malthouse

The
· Transport ·
Treasury

ISBN 978-1-913251-03-1

First Published in 2020 by Transport Treasury Publishing Ltd. 16 Highworth Close, High Wycombe, HP13 7PJ

www.ttpublishing.co.uk

Printed in the UK by Henry Ling Limited, at the Dorset Press, Dorchester. DT1 1HD.

Contents

Front cover: If a single image was to encapsulate the very essence of the Great Western at Swindon Works, then this cameo of No 6003 *King George IV* on 13 May 1955 is surely it. The immaculate Collett 4-6-0 stands ex-works alongside the iconic southern elevation of 'A' Shop having just received a Heavy Intermediate overhaul. The King had been 'inside' for just over a month and has received a four-row superheated WB boiler, fitted with a non-standard taller single chimney without the usual capuchon. It will shortly be paired with 4000 gallon tender No 2776, before a return to its home shed Old Oak Common. Note also the surviving external gas lamp above the locomotive's safety valve bonnet, supplied from the Gasworks located at the northern edge of the site. *RCR 5001-6100 (1075)*

Title page: This is a scene typical of the sidings situated to the western edge of the Swindon Works complex and an obvious highlight for many enthusiast's visits. Standing in the company of a solitary steel bodied mineral wagon on 17 January 1946 are a collection of William Dean's finest: (l-r) 2721 Class 0-6-0PT Nos 2765 and 2732, Dean Goods Class 0-6-0 Nos 2381 and 2406, Bulldog Class 4-4-0 No 3389 and Dean Goods No 2395. All of these locomotives were casualties of the mass withdrawals that took place in the weeks following the cessation of hostilities in September 1945. *RCR R1-1678 (697)*

Opposite: On what is believed to be one of Dick's final visits to Swindon Works to observe steam on 16 August 1964, he captured Churchward 28xx Class 2-8-0 No 2818 stood in a forlorn withdrawn state alongside the Iron Foundry. But this was not to be the end of the road for this December 1905 built locomotive, as it had been identified for potential preservation by the British Transport Commission since as early as 1953. Selected by nature of it being the last surviving example from the first batch of twenty 28xx type that retained inside steam pipes and the original stepped drop-end running plate. After being moved around the Swindon site for a number of years, it was to be eventually cosmetically restored at Eastleigh Works in 1966 to become part of the National Collection. At the time of writing, 2818 resides a matter of metres away from the location of the photograph, within STEAM - Museum of the Great Western Railway. Looking west towards Bristol, this vista also shows many of the key buildings at this end of the complex. Through the open ended Reception Shed, in the distance can be seen the Weighbridge House, with alongside the famous side profile of the huge 'A' Shop. Adjacent to the locomotive is the Pattern Store with its rooftop water tanks and the corner of the 'J' Shop Foundry, which now forms part of the McArthurGlen Shopping Outlet. *RCR R17501 (200)*

Rear cover: Dick Riley captured this stunning broadside portrait of a resplendent ex-works Churchward Mogul 2-6-0 No 5330 at the entrance throat to Swindon shed on Sunday 25 August 1957. The locomotive is fresh from its final Heavy General overhaul which concluded with the application of fully lined green paint and the late British Railways crest on the 3500gal tender. An imminent return to its home shed of Didcot awaits, from where 5330 was a regular performer over the Didcot, Newbury and Southampton line. The building in the background is the 1896 built General Stores, which was internally rail served, and from outside of which a subway under the Gloucester lines connected to the General Offices and Locomotive Works. *RCR R10801-11800 (367)*

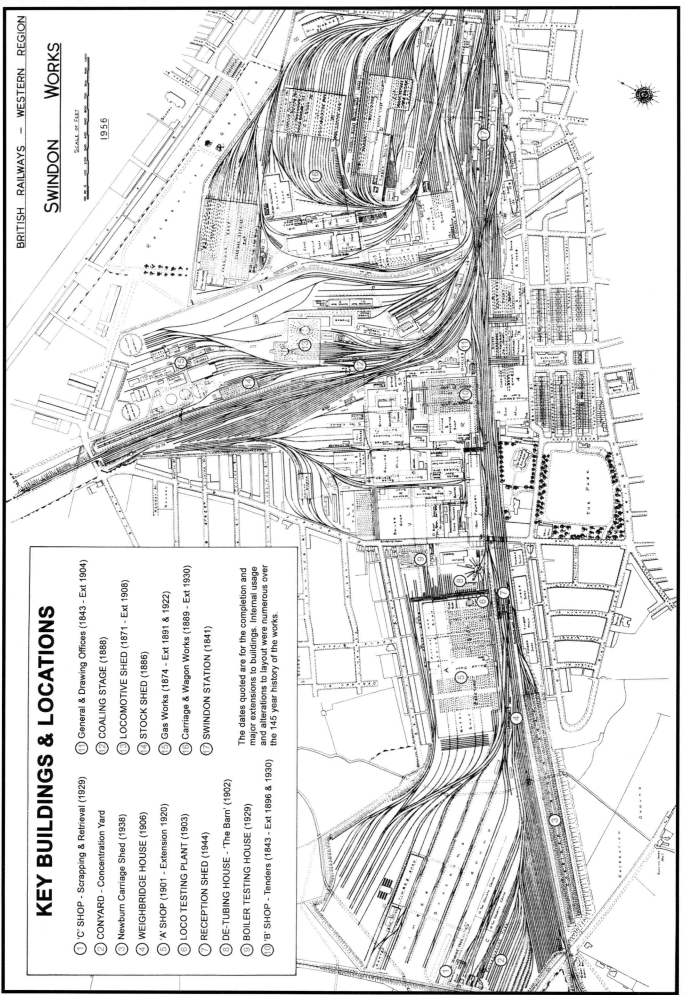

KEY BUILDINGS & LOCATIONS

1. 'C' SHOP - Scrapping & Retrieval (1929)
2. CONYARD - Concentration Yard
3. Newburn Carriage Shed (1938)
4. WEIGHBRIDGE HOUSE (1906)
5. 'A' SHOP (1901 - Extension 1920)
6. LOCO TESTING PLANT (1903)
7. RECEPTION SHED (1944)
8. DE-TUBING HOUSE - 'The Barn' (1902)
9. BOILER TESTING HOUSE (1929)
10. 'B' SHOP - Tenders (1843 - Ext 1896 & 1930)
11. General & Drawing Offices (1843 - Ext 1904)
12. COALING STAGE (1888)
13. LOCOMOTIVE SHED (1871 - Ext 1908)
14. STOCK SHED (1886)
15. Gas Works (1874 - Ext 1891 & 1922)
16. Carriage & Wagon Works (1889 - Ext 1930)
17. SWINDON STATION (1841)

The dates quoted are for the completion and major extensions to buildings. Internal usage and alterations to layout were numerous over the 145 year history of the works.

Swindon Works Plan (1956): Highlighting the key buildings and locations that feature in the Dick Riley photographs.

Introduction

The work of R C 'Dick' Riley is as noted for its diversity as it is for quantity, quality and historical importance. How fortunate we are that his desire to travel and record the later years of steam's dominance across the British railway network has bestowed such a rich archive. When assessing the vast collection of photographs he captured, it is evident though that certain locations held an enduring allure, resulting in repeated visits over the years. Foremost amongst these places was Swindon, the beating heart of the Great Western Empire and hub of its engineering enterprise. Between the years 1937 – 1964, Dick entered the vast works site on at least twenty-five occasions armed with his camera and it is this collection of imagery that forms the basis for this volume.

The thrill of exploring a large railway works was truly an assault on the senses, from viewing the mass concentration of locomotives in varying states of repair, to the pervading smell of engineering oils and varnish, and the all encompassing noise of heavy industry and machinery. These sights and sounds have been an addictive draw for railway enthusiasts for generations and Dick Riley was no exception, be it on the regular Wednesday and Sunday public openings or via the restricted access he gained through his network of contacts in the industry. Where his work differed from the majority was in its regard for the diversity of the environment, devoting as much attention on the old and the mundane as on the shiny and the new. This was no mean feat in a location where gleaming ex-works locomotives rightly demanded the spotlight.

As a professional photographer myself for the last 30 years, it is perhaps understandable that I took a particular interest in the technical aspects of the photographic collection. It is recorded that the earliest railway images captured by Dick Riley were taken on an ageing Box Brownie, which was in turn replaced by a basic Kodak Folding Camera some time in 1937. It is evident that creating these first photographs (featured in Chapter 1) was beset with focus issues caused by the quality of his lens and focal plane alignment. Despite these mechanical imperfections with his equipment, he was developing an eye for the subject matter and its composition, and this alone makes them worthy of inclusion. Things were to improve significantly with the purchase of a Zeiss Ikonta in 1946, equipped with a 75mm lens and capable of 1/125 of a second shutter speed. This coincided with the release of Ilford FP3 film (in 120 roll format), which he was to use extensively for black and white work from then on. Whilst only available in 40 ASA to begin with, by 1960 this had increased to 125 ASA with much improved grain structure. The later images featured in this album were taken on an Agfa Record III Camera, featuring an excellent 105mm lens and 1/250 shutter. The improvement is clearly evident as equipment, skill and experience had resulted in him becoming one of the finest proponents of his art in the country. It is worth noting at this point that from late 1954 onwards Dick was also using 35mm colour transparency film in a second camera, and readers may recognise previously published versions of some photographs he duplicated on Kodachrome. It is suggested that he created a frame to hold both cameras, in order to facilitate simultaneous exposures onto each format.

Swindon Works was indeed a magical place and not just to the generations who worked 'inside' the boundary walls. From its full time opening on 2 January 1843 to its final closure on 31 March 1986, the diverse activity that took place across the sprawling estate had a justified reputation for engineering excellence. Many quipped that there was the 'Swindon Way and the Wrong Way' and that most locomotives arrived at Swindon for overhaul in a better mechanical condition than the ex-works products of other railway companies! Such was the professionalism of the workforce and the quality of the Great Western Railway's designs. What is for certain is that the Locomotive, Carriage & Wagon Works, which at its height employed over 10,000 people, covered 326 acres of land and internally encompassed some 91 miles of track, was a world leading railway facility. Whilst many of the images that Dick captured during the years of his regular visits to Swindon could be viewed as traditional locomotive portraits, they also record the surroundings and atmosphere that were at its core. Hopefully the reader will enjoy this historical journey, courtesy of Mr. R C Riley, back to the time when Steam was King and Swindon was its Palace.

Andrew Malthouse
Ovington, Norfolk 2020.

Above: One of the earliest photographs captured by Dick Riley within the vast expanse of Swindon Works was this example dating from June 1937, when he was still in his mid-teens. Former Railway Operating Division (ROD) 2-8-0 No 3034 stands in the company of Dean 2021 Class 0-6-0PT No 2040 outside the Stock Shed. The Great Western's involvement with the Robinson designed ex-ROD locomotives is a complicated affair and beyond the scope of this caption, but this example was constructed by the North British Locomotive Company Ltd at their Queens Park Works in 1918, for intended war use. Coming into GWR stock in December 1926, it had been partially 'Swindonised' by the time of the photograph, including top feed, whistles, buffers and removal of the piston tail rods. The original smoke box door, chimney and tender however, pay homage to its Great Central design roots. Surviving into British Railways ownership, it was eventually withdrawn in February 1953. *RCR R1-1678 (242)*

Opposite top: The Riley collection bears testament to his fascination in recording locomotives of pre-Grouping heritage, and no location was richer in such subject matter during his early visits than the storage sidings in the Concentration Yard. It is easy to see why he would have been drawn to capture the last remaining ex Midland & South Western Junction Railway 0-6-0 goods engine No 1005. One of an eventual order of ten locomotives constructed by Beyer Peacock, it was delivered to the M&SWJR as their No 21 in 1899. Following Grouping and renumbering as 1005, this engine was the first of the class to be rebuilt with a Standard No 10 boiler and a Churchward style cab in January 1925. The remainder were similarly treated over the next couple of years and in this form, they became the first Great Western taper-boilered 0-6-0's. Already devoid of its tender, which was stored in a separate area of the dump, 1005 awaits the inevitable attention of the breakers. Although the records state an official withdrawal date of March 1938, this image is thought to have been taken during a visit on 20 February. *RCR R1-1678 (227)*

This page, bottom: On 6 April 1938 brand new 8750 Class 0-6-0PT No 3766 appears to be engaged on West End Station Pilot duties, with the Carriage & Wagon Works Offices and No 15 Machine Shop as a backdrop. Local employment such as this link was often utilised to run in ex-works tank locomotives, before either storage in the Stock Shed or despatch to their first allocated depot. *RCR R1-1678 (239)*

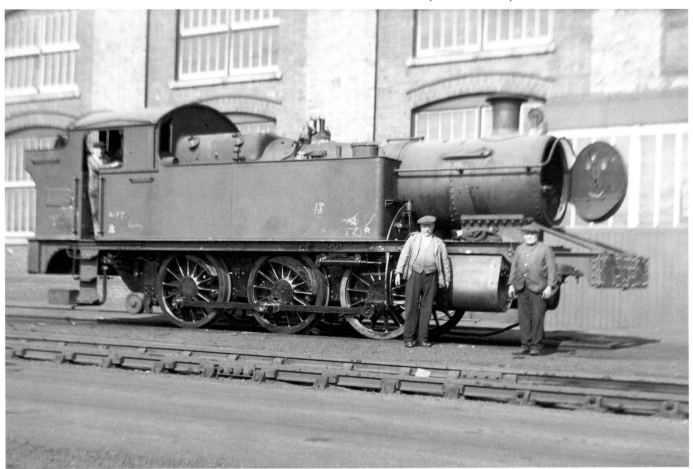

Opposite top: 28xx Class 2-8-0 No 2871 stands on one of the spur sidings off the 65ft turntable. Still ostensibly in the condition it was built in November 1918, with an inside steam piped boiler, lamp iron on top of the smokebox and tall safety valve bonnet. The Automatic Train Control apparatus (fitted to the entire class in 1930-31) can be clearly seen below the coupling hook. 6 April 1938. *RCR R1-1678 (231)*

Opposite bottom: During his visit to the Works on 6 April 1938, Dick understandably exposed a couple of frames of film on 'Buffalo' Class 0-6-0PT No 1620, as it engaged in shunting the reception sidings. This outside framed veteran was already 58 years old, having been originally built as a saddle tank in April 1880. Rebuilt with panniers in November 1917 and receiving an enclosed cab during 1926, it was taken out of normal service from Swindon shed in November 1937. Its presence still in operation some months later, is explained by the practice of utilising withdrawn but not yet condemned tank engines on Works Pilot duties until their boiler certificates expired. *RCR R1-1678 (232)*

Above: Despite the photographic deficiencies that Dick experienced with his earlier Kodak cameras, this image of 45xx Small Prairie No 4532 standing alongside 'A' Shop on 6 April 1938 has to be included for its novelty value alone. The 2-6-2T is clearly mid way through overhaul, with the bottom end partially completed and undergoing a rolling test or move to another part of the Works complex. Quite how the duty 'Works Pilot' engine assisted with the movement of partially complete locomotives in this state is open to speculation, although capstans were also strategically placed around the site for such eventualities. No 4532 was one of the third batch of Churchward's highly successful 45xx Class, built to Lot.191 in 1913. Following this current overhaul, transfer to Bristol Bath Road shed took place on the 28 May 1938. It was destined to be a well-travelled locomotive, being resident at nine different sheds before removal from service in February 1955. Final cutting took place at Swindon within a month of withdrawal, having attained a recorded mileage of 1,079,753. *RCR R1-1678 (244)*

Above: Brand new Collett 2884 Class 2-8-0 No 2890 stands on the road outside the eastern entrance to the Weighbridge building on 6 April 1938. The wall and lamp to the right mark the steps to a subway under the main running lines to 'Newburn House' the residence of the GWR's Chief Mechanical Engineer, which was to be demolished later in the year to make way for a new carriage shed. The attendant crew and fitters have either just removed or are about to take the locomotive onto the weighbridge for final checks prior to its release to traffic two days later. Resplendent in pre-war green livery and adorned with the GWR 'shirt button' monogram on its tender, some of the modifications from Churchward's original 28xx design can be seen, including outside steam pipes, fire iron tunnel on the running plate and the modern side-window cab. This heavy freight stalwart was to go on to have a service life of just short of 27 years. *RCR R1-1678 (234)*

Opposite: With the western end of 'A' Shop and the travelling crane in the background, 1854 Class 0-6-0PT No 1797 is pictured on the headshunt access to the Weighbridge building. The ex-works locomotive is either destined for weighing, or is possibly undergoing running tests to bed in and check the motion and springs. For tank engines this process took place from here along sidings the full length of the Locomotive Works to the Main Office buildings, whereas larger locomotives were assigned a short running in turn on the main line. Built as a saddle tank to a William Dean design in June 1895, 1797 was rebuilt as a pannier tank under Churchward's tenure in December 1922. Further modifications are evident following this recent overhaul, including a superheated boiler, parallel Collett buffers and enlarged bunker, but interestingly it has retained its open cab. A long time St Blazey resident, it was destined for final withdrawal from the Cornish shed in July 1946, having given over 51 years service to the GWR. 6 April 1938. *RCR R1-1678 (245)*

Opposite top: Dick Riley's desire to record the unusual is typified by this portrait of the unique 0-4-0ST No 45, taken amongst the long line of locomotives awaiting disposal in the Conyard dump. Unusually on this occasion he did not record the date in his trusty notebook (which can be seen placed in the foreground), but it is thought to be during the visit on 6 April 1938, which coincides with the locomotive's withdrawal. Built at Wolverhampton in June 1880 as replacement for an ageing Shrewsbury & Birmingham Railway shunting engine, No 45 held claim to being the only conventional design 0-4-0ST constructed in a GWR works. Apart from the addition of a cab, it remained in almost original condition, operating for the majority of its life from Croes Newydd shed in Wrexham. This characterful little engine accrued a mere 430,000 miles during a 58-year service career. *RCR R1-1678 (236)*

Opposite bottom: A little further along the scrap line from the previous image we find ex M&SWJR 4-4-0 No 1123. Constructed by the North British Locomotive Company as its first owner's No 5 in April 1912, it was rebuilt with a Standard No 2 boiler at Swindon in August 1929. The elegant design seems somewhat spoilt by the oversize copper capped chimney and tall safety valve bonnet. The locomotive's original six-wheeled tender had already been removed and was to see further service following alteration to a water tank. *RCR R1-1678 (237)*

Above: During a visit on 15 August 1938, Star Class 4-6-0 No 4071 *Cleeve Abbey* is captured adjacent to the De-Tubing House, locally referred to as 'The Barn'. Built in February 1923 as the penultimate Star, it was one of ten locomotives from the last batch (4063-4072) selected for rebuilding into Castles (5083-5092). Although officially classed by the GWR as renewals, so as to attract a Government Grant to fund the work, this accounts for the allocation of new numbers as opposed to the five earlier Star rebuilds that retained their original identity. *Cleeve Abbey* had just arrived at Swindon from Bristol Bath Road shed and following assessment is about to undergo stripping, firstly in the De-Tubing House before final dismantling inside 'A' Shop, a process that culminated in its official withdrawal as a Star in early September. The resurrection into Castle Class No 5091 was completed by 18 December 1938 and a release to traffic saw the 'new' engine return to Bath Road. Latterly converted to oil burning between August 1946 and October 1948, the distinguished history of this locomotive was to come to an end with final withdrawal on 3 October 1964. *RCR R1-1678 (270)*

Above: 43xx Class 2-6-0 No 4394 stands alongside the Test House, at the eastern end of the 'A' Shop complex on 15 August 1938. The huge success of these versatile moguls resulted in them becoming Churchward's most numerous class, with 342 examples constructed to a similar basic design between 1911 and 1932. Dating from September 1916, this locomotive has just been withdrawn from revenue service and is about to undergo the now established process of dismantling, to provide wheels and motion parts for new Grange and Manor 4-6-0s. From here it would be moved via the traverser into the De-Tubing House for boiler stripping, before transfer to the main erecting shop for the aforementioned parts to be extracted and refurbished. Finally the remaining frames and cylinders would be loaded onto a flat wagon for the move to 'C' Shop and cutting. Although it is not recorded exactly which locomotive was to receive these donor parts, it would have almost certainly been one of the last batch of Granges (6860-6879) constructed between February and May 1939. *RCR R1-1678 (271)*

Opposite top: On 15 August 1938, Churchward 3150 Class 2-6-2T No 3173, has returned to its October 1907 birthplace. Having just arrived from Wolverhampton Stafford Road shed, it is about to enter 'A' Shop for major rebuilding into the first of the Collett 31xx Class (see page 16). Following this transformation it was to return to former haunts at Gloucester, employed banking trains up the climb from Brimscombe to Sapperton Tunnel. *RCR R1-1678 (268)*

Opposite bottom: Also on 15 August 1938, Dick captured this scene on the scrap line that would surely have modern day preservationists running for their chequebooks! Dean Bulldog Class 4-4-0 No 3330 *Orion* sits awaiting its final attention from the Swindon workforce. One of the last curved frame Bulldogs to remain in traffic, *Orion* dated from February 1900 and was initially No 3342, before its identity change as part of the 1912-renumbering programme. Withdrawn from Bristol St Philips Marsh shed having accrued 1,121,099 miles, the locomotive appears to have arrived for scrapping coupled to a very late surviving Armstrong 2500-gallon double-framed tender. *RCR R1-1678 (269)*

Left: Another unusual subject to attract attention during a 27 November 1938 visit, was 4-wheel 'Simplex' petrol shunter No 15. The GWR purchased five similar vehicles from the Motor Rail and Tram Company Ltd of Bedford, between 1923 and 1927. No 15 was the first of these, coming into stock and allocated to the Goods Department at Wednesbury in April 1923. It later saw use at Bridgwater Docks and at Taunton, before being recorded as 'laid up as spare' in 1938, which would explain its presence at Swindon. It was destined for a return to service, before final withdrawal and disposal in March 1951. Despite the poor quality of the image, it is possible to discern the warning bell and standard GW numberplate, which only adorned this example, as the other four had their identity simply painted on. *RCR R1-1678 (117)*

Opposite bottom: Occupying one of the construction bays within the (AE) Erecting section of the cavernous 'A' Shop, we see 2-6-2T No 3100 taking shape on 27 November 1938. The locomotive is actually a rebuild using the frames from former 3150 Class No 3173, and was the first of a Government Grant funded scheme to convert all forty-one 3150s to modern standards. The onset of war in September 1939 halted the programme, with only five locomotives (3100-3104) having undergone the transformation. The refurbished bunker can be seen on the left and the recycled frames have been adorned with new cylinders and front end, smaller 5'3" coupled wheels and a brand new 225 psi boiler. Intended for banking and pilot duties, 3100 was released to traffic just over a month after the photograph and would remain in traffic until May 1957. *RCR R1-1678 (115)*

Above: By late 1938, probably encouraged by the increasing ASA speed of film stock available, Dick began to attempt more internal images. Typical is this 27 November 1938 example, as he recorded 28xx Class 2-8-0 No 2878 receiving an Intermediate overhaul inside 'A' Shop. Built in February 1919 as part of Lot. 210, 2878 was one of the post-war final batch of Churchward locomotives. All of its wheels, motion parts and pistons have been removed to be engineered remotely in the (AW) Wheel and (AM) Machine areas of the Shop respectively. The removal of the firebox cladding suggests attention is also required in this area, with apparent scant regard given to disturbing the asbestos lagging beneath! *RCR R1-1678 (277)*

Above: Newly constructed Collett 8750 Class 0-6-0PT No 3796, stands on the holding sidings at the eastern end of 'A' Shop on 27 November 1938. The little workhorse was to be imminently despatched to Newport Ebbw Junction shed, where it was to remain for the next fifteen years before transfer to the delights of South Devon and Newton Abbot in 1953. A return to South Wales for the final two years of its life preceded withdrawal in March 1965, and the cutter's torch at Cashmore's yard in Newport. *RCR R1-1678 (109)*

Opposite top: On 26 February 1939, Collett Grange Class 4-6-0 No 6866 *Morfa Grange* nears the final stage of its construction in 'A' Shop as part of Lot.308. Utilising the wheels and motion from withdrawn Churchward 2-6-0s, but with new cylinder blocks and Standard No 1 boilers (as used on the Halls), the Granges were amongst the most successful of all Swindon products. The eventual class of eighty locomotives were to cost on average less than £4000 each, testament to the efficiency of the mass engineering production undertaken by the Great Western. *Morfa Grange* was to be delivered to Tyseley shed just over a month after this photograph was taken, and was to remain in traffic until 27 May 1965, before being broken up at Cashmore's scrapyard in Great Bridge. *RCR R1-1678 (116)*

Opposite bottom: ROD 2-8-0 No 3020 undergoes a boiler in the frames overhaul in the Erecting Shop on 26 February 1939. The front pony truck and two driving axles have been removed and attention is being given to the lower section of the copper firebox. The RODs were altered to varying degrees over a number of years by the Great Western and whilst this example retains its original smokebox door, it has received the later 47xx type chimney. Built by the North British Locomotive Company in 1919 as ROD No 1794, this locomotive was purchased by the GWR in 1925 and released into traffic during April 1926. It was to be withdrawn from service in June 1954. *RCR R1-1678 (139)*

Above: Earl Class 4-4-0 No 3224 stands on the sidings alongside 'B' Shop, following completion on 26 February 1939. This handsome class of lightweight outside framed locomotives were classified as new builds, although as 3224 had received the boiler from Duke Class No 3290 and frames from Bulldog No 3409, it could be more accurately described as a rebuild. Outshopped between 1936-1939, the twenty-nine strong class were initially referred to as 'Earls' in recognition of the first thirteen carrying the names of members of the peerage. Following the plates being removed in June 1937 for transfer to Castle class locomotives (5043-5055), they were latterly re-christened 'Dukedogs'. Subsequently renumbered 9024 in September 1946, this engine was to spend the majority of its working life on the Central Wales Division. Firstly operating from Shrewsbury shed and finally Machynlleth, from where it was withdrawn in September 1957. *RCR R1-1678 (127)*

Opposite top: The imposing bulk of Collett 72xx Class 2-8-2T No 7250 is captured on the sidings adjacent to 'A' Shop on 26 February 1939. Following the end of the Great Depression, there was an increasing need for more powerful locomotives with greater endurance to haul long distance coal trains from South Wales into England. To meet this requirement between 1934-1939, fifty-four 2-8-0Ts were rebuilt with extended bunkers and supporting rear radial axles. Converted from Churchward 42xx No 4219 of December 1912, 7250 was from the third and final batch where the water tank was increased to 2,700 gallons at the expense of coal capacity being reduced to 5 tons. This is distinguished by the angled line of rivets running above the numberplate, as opposed to below on the earlier batches of rebuilds. The locomotive is probably engaged in running-in trials prior to its release to traffic. Unusually it was to have an allocation history not dominated by South Wales sheds, spending time at Newton Abbot, St Philips Marsh and Worcester, before withdrawal on 28 September 1964. *RCR R1-1678 (133)*

Opposite bottom: Star Class 4-6-0 No 4012 *Knight of the Thistle* stands on the reception siding alongside the Test House, awaiting entry into the Works for attention on 26 February 1939. One of Churchward's elegant four-cylinder express passenger locomotives, 4012 was part of the second batch built to Lot.173 in March 1908 and named after Knights of the realm. The Order of the Thistle is the greatest level of chivalry in Scotland, comprising of a maximum of sixteen Knights appointed by the Sovereign. Destined for a further ten years of revenue earning service, the engine was withdrawn from Newton Abbot shed in October 1949 and scrapped back at its birthplace of Swindon. To the rear can be seen the shallow pit and twin booms of the electric traverser table, which sits just out of shot to the right. The end wall of the De-Tubing House beyond has yet to receive the covered awning, prominent in later images taken around this location. *RCR R1-1678 (134)*

Opposite top: Manor Class 4-6-0 No 7815 *Fritwell Manor* is just over one month old when captured at the southern entrance to the Locomotive Shed yard on 26 February 1939. Its external condition suggests it has been in regular traffic for some days, and it was to remain at Swindon for a few more weeks before moving to its first home at Gloucester. The Manors were to be Collett's final class of 4-6-0s and incorporated the specially designed Standard No 14 boiler. Like the Granges, they utilised wheels and motion from withdrawn 43xx locomotives (in this case No 4360) and were paired with refurbished Churchward 3500-gallon tenders. The house after which 7815 was named is situated five miles north west of Bicester in Oxfordshire, and was owned by Margaret Boleyn, grandmother of Anne Boleyn, the second wife of King Henry VIII. In the background beyond the main lines to Gloucester, 36-ton Ransomes & Rapier steam breakdown crane No 2 of 1908, can be seen stabled in its usual siding. *RCR R1-1678 (130)*

Opposite bottom: On 17 January 1946, Dean 1854 Class 0-6-0PT No 1751 and George Armstrong 517 Class 0-4-2T No 1161 stand forlornly on the dump sidings in the Conyard. Withdrawn locomotives were temporarily stored on these long sidings before being called forward to enter 'C' Shop for parts retrieval, cutting and sorting into reusable metal consignments. Built in October 1892 as a saddle tank, 1751 converted to pannier tank configuration with a diagram B4 boiler (back dome Belpaire) in August 1932. Later modifications also included superheating and an enlarged bunker, but as can be seen this example never received the enclosed cab bestowed upon some of the class. It could be argued that the 156 strong 517 Class collectively form one of the most complex of all Great Western locomotive histories. 1161 was built in February 1876 at Wolverhampton and the many modifications over its lifetime include the installation of Auto Apparatus in June 1918 and the fitting of a BR4 Belpaire boiler, Collett cab and bunker in May 1924. It was first removed from service in April 1939, but re-instated in February 1940 as part of wartime measures. Final withdrawal from Swindon shed came in October 1945, one of the last handful of the class to succumb. *RCR R1-1678 (695)*

Above: Also recorded on the scrap line on 17 January 1946 was another 1854 and 517 Class pairing. No 1899 dated from August 1895 and received its pannier tanks in November 1911, the worn paint on which reveal both Great Western and later 'Shirtbutton' markings. The 0-4-2T No 1436 retained the short wheelbase it was built with in November 1877, and as both locomotives had been out of service for over a year, it would appear the deluge of late wartime withdrawals was beginning to cause a backlog for the Swindon cutters. *RCR R1-1678 (696)*

23

Opposite: On his visit to Swindon Works on 29 May 1946, Dick was attracted to record the in steam ex-works Collett 48xx 0-4-2T No 4869. The February 1936 vintage engine had just been released from a General overhaul, which had taken just over four weeks to complete. Its original short whistle shield has been replaced with a standard longer version and it looks a picture in plain green adorned with the last style of GWR insignia. Soon to be renumbered 1468 in the coming November, this little autotank was to spend the entirety of its 23 year life allocated to Exeter, as denoted by the EXE on the side footstep.

To the rear of the locomotive we can observe the profile of 'A' Shop as it was developed. Right of the bunker is the original 1901 building, with the extension completed in 1920 directly behind. Constructed from smooth faced 'Cattybrook' red brick with blue brick footings and pillars, the huge structure became an iconic symbol of Great Western engineering prowess and with a covered area in excess of 11 acres, one of the largest such facilities in the world. *RCR R1-1678 (703)*

Above: Newly constructed Collett Castle Class 4-6-0 No 7001 *Denbigh Castle* is heading light engine on the Up Main Line adjacent to the Works on 29 May 1946, possibly undergoing running trials or transfer to Swindon locomotive shed prior to despatch to its first home at Cardiff Canton. The immaculate engine wears the post-war fully lined green livery, with the G (Crest) W emblem adorning the 4000-gallon tender (No 4013). It was to be renamed *Sir James Milne* in February 1948, two months after Nationalisation, in recognition of the final General Manager of the Great Western Railway. 7001 was the third Castle to carry the name of the mighty North Wales fortress, following 5049 and 5074 before transfer for a final time to 7032 in June 1950.

In the background can be seen part of the huge Newburn Carriage Sheds, built in 1938 and still daubed in its distinctive wartime camouflage paint, and the rooftops of the worker's houses in Dean Street. *RCR R1-1678 (704)*

Above: Collett 8750 Class 0-6-0PT No 9648 engages in a spot of shunting adjacent to 'A' Shop on 29 May 1946. Although only completed a few weeks previously, the presence of the pep pipe hanging down from the footplate and the staining on the tank sides suggest it has already been put to work. Interestingly the Engine History card for this locomotive indicates its arrival at Cardiff Canton shed on 25 May, but this classic Riley portrait proves it lingered in Wiltshire a while longer. What is certain is that it was to spend its entire 18-year life allocated to sheds in South Wales. *RCR R1-1678 (707)*

Left: By the time of Dick's visit on 29 May 1946, 1854 Class 0-6-0PT No 1751 had moved from the works dump (see page 22) to the sidings outside 'A' Shop. This was possibly for parts retrieval as evidenced by the missing dome top and telltale fitter's chalk marks. This locomotive was one of sixty-four of the class fitted for Automatic Train Control, the shoe for which is visible under the bunker. Withdrawn from Newton Abbot the previous November (the NA allocation lettering is just discernable on the running plate below the front sandbox), a final journey to 'C' Shop for cutting was surely only weeks away. *RCR R1-1678 (709)*

Above: Encountered during a private visit on Thursday 16 February 1950 was a rare survivor in the shape of 3571 Class 0-4-2T No 3574. Built between 1895-1897 to a George Armstrong design at Wolverhampton, the ten members of the class were a development of the 517s, featuring unique framing at the trailing end and larger boilers. Most of the class were employed on local passenger workings in the north west extremities of the Great Western territory, although this example spent the later part of its life on carriage shunting work around Worcester. The last to be withdrawn in December 1949, 3574 had also been unique in retaining the numberplate centrally on its tanksides, somewhat disrupting the GWR branding.
RCR 2199-3948 (294)

Above: Another Armstrong rarity to attract attention on the Swindon Works dump was 850 Class 0-6-0ST No 2007. Built at Wolverhampton in October 1892, this was one of only two to survive into British Railways days still in saddle tank configuration. Apart from the enlarged bunker, this locomotive is externally remarkably unaltered from its as built condition. Confusion often reigns over the design attribution of the 170 strong 850 Class, as whilst penned by George Armstrong at Wolverhampton, he was officially subservient to his brother Joseph at Swindon, and to complicate matters further the post-1877 built locomotives were constructed under William Dean's tenure. 16 February 1950. *RCR 2199-3948 (301)*

Opposite top: The 645 Class were another design of Wolverhampton 0-6-0 saddle tank that were later rebuilt with panniers. No 1542 was constructed in February 1880 and transformed into the state depicted here in March 1928. One of only four that survived into BR stock, it appears to have been in the wars judging by the bent handrail and substantial tank patch repair. Not deemed worthy of a smokebox number by its new owners, it has at least received the short-lived British Railways lettering in the GWR Egyptian font style over its worn green paintwork. Remaining a resident of Swindon shed until withdrawal a year after this 16 February 1950 photograph was taken, this loco was regularly employed on the Conyard or Sawmill Pilot links, as identified by the solitary lamp and attendant shunter's truck. *RCR 2199-3948 (305)*

Opposite bottom: Viewed through the open side of the Reception Shed on 11 June 1950, we find new build Hawksworth 16xx Class 0-6-0PT No 1620. The lightweight pannier is about to be coaled and watered in the adjacent shed prior to some gentle running in along the three-quarter mile 'Factory Siding'.
It was standard practice for a receiving running shed to apply the respective new shedplate to the lower smokebox door, but it is interesting to note that the Swindon painters were persisting with the traditional stencils of the previous regime, seen here on the front sandbox. As indicated, the locomotive's first allocation was to be Cardiff East Dock (C.E.D) five days later, but it moved on to Abercynon (88E) within a month, where it remained for the rest of its criminally short ten year existence. Officially condemned on 8 June 1960 and sold to R.S. Hayes Ltd in Bridgend for disposal, it was reduced to scrap metal during March 1961. *RCR 2199-3948 (320)*

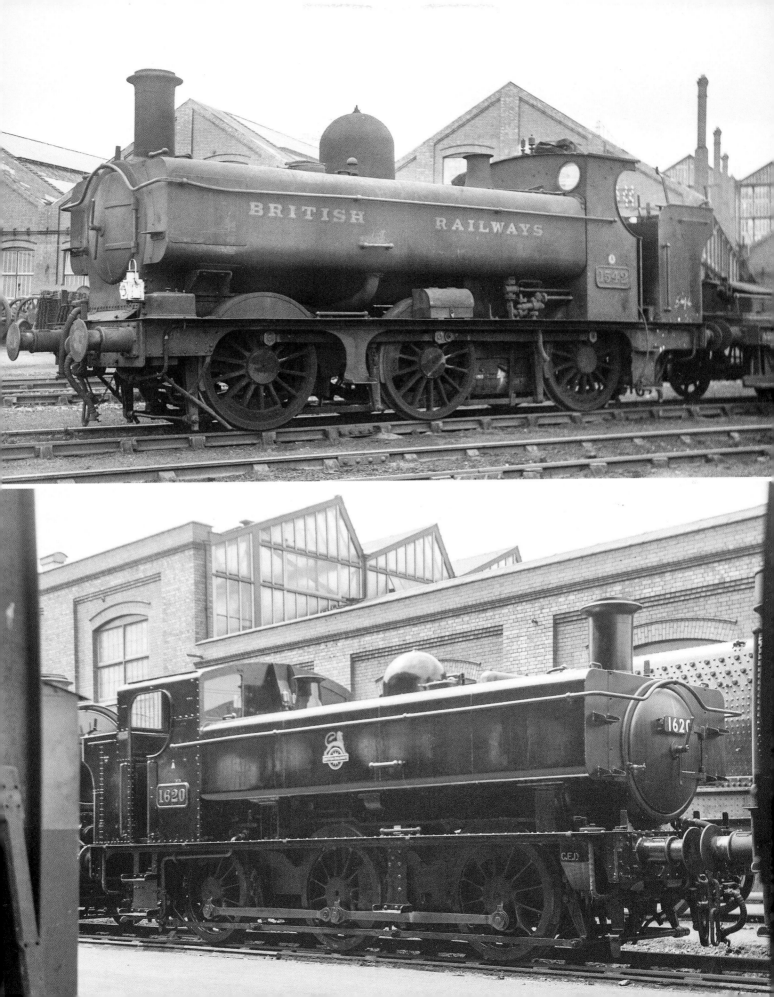

Above: A stranger in the camp is captured on 11 June 1950, in the shape of ex-LMS Ivatt Class 2 2-6-0 No 46413. Built at Crewe in February 1947 as one of the first batch of twenty locomotives built under the auspices of the old company, it is interesting to note the LMS lettering still adorning the tender side. Its presence at Swindon can be explained by a loan to the Western Region between 16 July 1949 and 9 September 1950 in order to undertake testing on both the stationary rollers in the Loco Test Plant and controlled road tests out on the main line. Much attention was paid to improving the draughting of these locomotives, a particular area of Swindon expertise, as can be evidenced by the test equipment in the chimney and on the front running plate. The Test Plant (on the right) was still utilised extensively following Nationalisation and was accessed via a traverser table, partly visible behind the tender. Whilst 46413 was returned to the London Midland Region and Blackpool Central (24E) shed, this was not to be Swindon's last association with the type, as the final batch of twenty-five locomotives (46503-46527) were constructed in the Works between November 1952 and April 1953 for use on the Western Region (see on page 50). *RCR 2199-3948 (316)*

Opposite top: Standing just to the right of the previous image and showing the entrance doors into the 1903 Locomotive Testing Plant building, is gleaming ex-works 14xx Class 0-4-2T No 1445. Built as No 4845 in April 1935 and renumbered on 23 November 1946, the engine had been in Swindon Works since 8 May 1950 undergoing a Heavy General overhaul. The records show as part of this work it has received the non-top feed fitted boiler (No 8066) and had accumulated 486,019 miles thus far. Return to its long-time home of Ross-on-Wye shed (a sub-shed of Hereford (85C) and still intact today as a delightful cafe) was to take place within days, to resume regular duties on the Ross-Monmouth auto workings. Occupying the south east corner of 'A' Shop, the Test Plant was originally planned to feature four rolling road test beds for differing wheelbases, but in the end provision was only made for the one bed with adjustable rollers. Additional wheel-drops were also provided in the first two bays, to allow comprehensive running-in and adjustment of high load bearings, axleboxes and springs. It is probable that 1445 has just made use of these facilities for final tweaks to be made prior to release to service. 11 June 1950. *RCR 2199-3948 (318)*

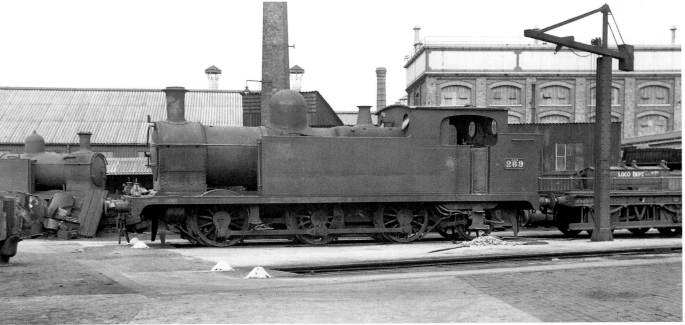

This page bottom: The practice of utilising withdrawn tank engines for 'Works Pilot' duties continued well into British Railways days, as evidenced by ex-Barry Railway B1 Class 0-6-2T No 269 on 11 June 1950. These absorbed South Wales tanks seem to have been particularly popular for this role, with Nos 203, 209, 211, 258, 272, 337, 344, 349, 383, 389, 397, 434 and 435 also known to have been employed before being ousted by modern panniers that had become surplus by the onset of dieselisation. This locomotive was delivered by the Sharp Stewart & Co Ltd as Barry Railway No 113 in June 1900, predominantly for hauling the endless cycle of mineral trains emanating from the South Wales Valleys down to Barry Docks for onward shipment. It became GWR No 269 at the Grouping in 1923 and was subsequently fitted with a non-superheated Standard No 9 boiler in January 1932, before eventual withdrawal from revenue service in October 1949. Behind the locomotive can be glimpsed the corrugated roof of the Mess Room on the left and the 1896 built Pattern Store with its 225,000 gallon rooftop water tanks, which survives intact to this day. *RCR 2199-3948 (319)*

Above: Churchward Saint Class 4-6-0 No 2934 *Butleigh Court* in British Railways mixed traffic lined black, stands in front of its home shed of Swindon on 11 June 1950. This somewhat camera shy Saint was built in November 1911 and was one of the class to receive a new front end with extended frames, new cylinders, parallel buffers and outside steam pipes in November 1938. Fresh from a recent Heavy Intermediate overhaul, its pleasing condition with red backed name and numberplates belie the fact it has only two years left in traffic. *RCR 2199-3948 (325)*

Opposite top: Also on 11 June 1950, Dick's inclination to record all things new prompted him to capture this shot of Hawksworth 94xx Class 0-6-0PT No 8460 stabled adjacent to Swindon shed coaling road. These powerful 4F rated locomotives were the final manifestation of the long lineage of GW 0-6-0 Pannier Tanks, with a total of 210 constructed between 1947-56 (the first ten at Swindon and the remainder by outside contractors). No 8460 was one of fifty built by the Yorkshire Engine Company at their Meadow Hall Works in Sheffield, whose oval builders plate can be seen affixed to the front splasher. In the days previous to the photograph the engine would have arrived at Swindon Works for acceptance examination and fitting of its coupling rods and ATC equipment, which usually took place in the old erecting shop area of 'B' Shop. Following the period of running trials in which it is currently engaged, it was dispatched on 17 June to its first allocation at Barry shed in South Wales. Note the higher than normal positioning of the smokebox numberplate. *RCR 2199-3948 (327)*

Opposite bottom: Collett 58xx Class 0-4-2T No 5804 stands awaiting signals at the west end of Swindon Station on 9 June 1951. One of the batch of twenty non-auto fitted versions of the 48xx Class, intended for branch and light shunting work. Built in January 1933, 5804 spent the majority of its working life allocated to Swindon shed, employed on the Malmesbury, Tetbury and Highworth branches, and as on this occasion, Station Pilot duties at Swindon. It was withdrawn in June 1959 and scrapped within 'C' Shop two months later. *RCR 2199-3948 (454)*

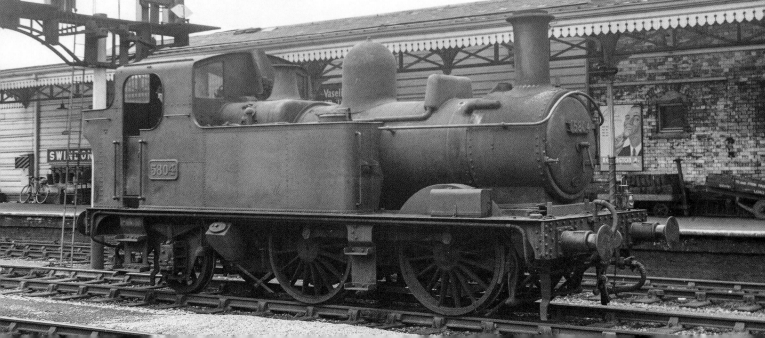

Opposite top: In the Conyard sidings on 9 June 1951 we find a pairing of withdrawn Churchward standard passenger 4-6-0s, in the form of four-cylinder Star No 4058 (formerly *Princess Augusta*) and two-cylinder Saint No 2947 (formerly *Madresfield Court*). Both locomotives had been removed from service two months previously from Wolverhampton Stafford Road and Swindon sheds respectively, having accumulated in excess of 1.6 million miles each. It is interesting to note that the sole remaining numberplate seen adorning the cabside of 2947 was sold at auction in January 2000 for over £2,500, a sum far greater than the whole scrap value of the locomotive in 1951! *RCR 2199-3948 (459)*

Opposite bottom: Pilot duties were not exclusively handled by withdrawn 0-6-2Ts during the early 1950s, as seen by Dean 1854 Class 0-6-0PT No 1709 stabled next to the Works turntable on Saturday 9 June 1951. Withdrawn from normal duties in November 1950, the sixty-year-old veteran was to spend a number of months working as both the 'A' and 'B' Shop Works Pilot prior to its final demise. Locomotives engaged on these duties were crewed and serviced by members of the Works BSE team and as such did not go to the Running Shed for attention. The telltale pile of ash indicates the in-situ cleaning of the firebox and was a familiar feature to be found around the turntable roads. *RCR 2199-3948 (468)*

Above: One of the other ex-Barry Railway B1 Class 0-6-2Ts used as a Works Pilot was No 272 of June 1900, which had been withdrawn in March 1950 from Barry shed. It is interesting to note it still retained the 'Grotesque' style of GWR lettering that was introduced during WW2 by Caerphilly Works. As previously seen it was common practice for the pilots to operate in tandem with a shunting truck, in this case No W94973, a Diagram M3 variant built in October 1917 to Lot. 841 and fitted with self-contained buffers. 9 June 1951. *RCR 2199-3948 (469)*

Opposite top: Fresh from attention in the nearby Works and apparently being gainfully employed on a running-in turn, Collett 61xx Class 2-6-2T No 6165 stands taking water next to the Coaling Stage at Swindon shed on 9 June 1951. The seventy strong 61xx sub-class of Large Prairies were specifically introduced for accelerated Paddington Suburban services from 1931 and were allocated across the London Division sheds. This particular example was from the last batch built in October 1935 and was a resident of Southall (81C) at the time of the photograph. It unusually carries a tall version of the safety valve bonnet. The 1888 built coaling facilities at Swindon occupied a restricted space between the shed yard and the Gloucester lines and as such featured an unusual end on loading bay at the southern end of the stage and a narrow brick and concrete elevated wagon road, rather than the more common earth mound ramp found at most sheds. *RCR 2199-3948 (470)*

Opposite bottom: Pictured berthed around one of the internal turntable roads inside Swindon shed on 9 June 1951, is ex-Swansea Harbour Trust 0-4-0ST No 1140. Supplied to the SHT as their No 5 in April 1905, the diminutive shunter featured 3'5" wheels and 14"x22" cylinders and was a product from the Kilmarnock Works of Andrew Barclay Sons & Co Ltd. Following the absorption of the SHT into the GWR on 1 July 1923 the locomotive was renumbered No 701 and acquired the distinctive GW style safety valve during the early 1930s. The final identity change to No 1140 took place in June 1948 and following this recent overhaul, it has received BR black paint, a smokebox door numberplate and Swansea East Dock (87D) shedplate. Note also the warning bell in front of the whistle, which was a common feature on most of the SHT locomotive fleet. It was to remain active in South Wales for a few more years, eventually withdrawn in May 1958. *RCR 2199-3948 (472)*

Above: Sunday 15 June 1952 was to be an unusually busy day at Swindon Works due to the arrival of the Stephenson Locomotive Society 'Saint Special', hauled by Churchward Saint Class 4-6-0 No 2920 *Saint David*. Destined to be the last of the class in service and operating from Hereford (85C) shed, *Saint David* gained celebrity status in its later years as the locomotive of choice on numerous enthusiast specials. This particular working had left Birmingham Snow Hill at 10:30am, stopping at Gloucester, before arriving at Swindon at 2:30pm. It is not certain whether Dick travelled on the train or followed its progress by road, but he did photograph the locomotive during its stopover at Gloucester (85B) shed earlier in the day, giving him just enough time to drive the 35 miles to catch up with it again at Swindon! Here we see the train alongside the Weighbridge House, having just traversed tender first from the Station in order to alight the passengers eager to visit the Works. The thought of allowing six coaches of railway enthusiasts to dismount a train so close to main running lines is today unthinkable. The train departed Rodbourne Lane at 6:00pm for the return journey to Birmingham, as can be seen on page 43. *RCR 2199-3948 (906)*

Above; Its days as a flagship of the Great Western Railway are a distant memory as Churchward Star Class 4-6-0 No 4050 (formerly *Princess Alice*) stands derelict in the Conyard sidings awaiting the inevitable end on 15 June 1952. Built at Swindon in June 1914 as part of Lot. 199, it was the first Star to be fitted with a speedometer (operating off the rear driving wheel) in late 1914. Elbow outside steam pipes were fitted in June 1946 and withdrawal from Landore (87E) came in February 1952 having run 1,706,323 miles. The build cost of £4,698 for the locomotive is somewhat dwarfed by the combined sum of £21,000 that the absent name and numberplate achieved at auction in 2004. Behind, 51xx Class 2-6-2T No 5144 (formerly No 3144) of March 1906, faces a similar fate in the nearby 'C' Shop. *RCR 2199-3948 (907)*

Opposite: A sister locomotive with a much brighter future than in the previous image is portrayed by No 4003 *Lode Star* undergoing initial preparation for preservation in one of the Testing Plant bays on 15 June 1952. There has been some confusion over the sequence of events surrounding the restoration of *Lode Star,* but as it was one of the last remaining 1907-built Stars in traffic, it had been earmarked for saving by the Western Region from as early as February 1951. Following withdrawal from Landore shed, it arrived back at Swindon on 18 July 1951 coupled to Collett 4000-gallon tender (No 2410), from which it was separated almost immediately. It was moved to various locations in and around 'A' Shop over the next 12 months, receiving some attention, such as removal of its BR smokebox numberplate and pairing with a Churchward 3,500-gallon tender (No 1726). It was then mothballed and placed into storage in the Stock Shed for a number of years (see page 70). Eventually a full restoration commenced in 'A' Shop in July 1961, which included backdating to near original condition including removal of the outside steampipes, before placement into the then Swindon Railway Museum in Faringdon Road on 29 April 1962. *RCR 2199-3948 (914)*

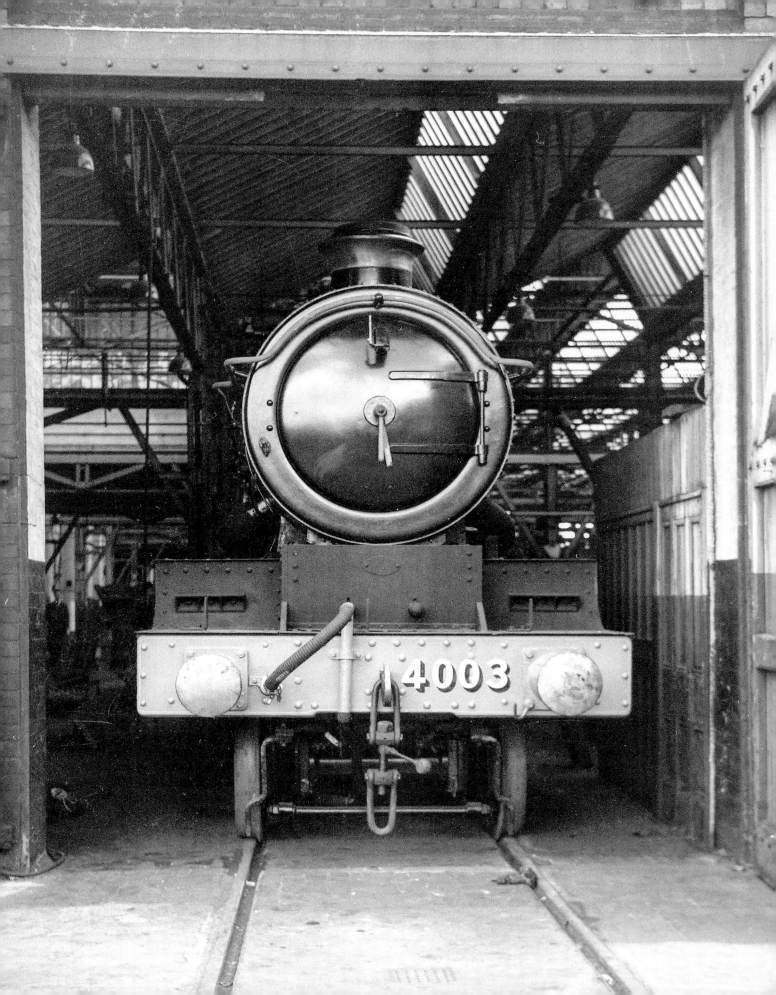

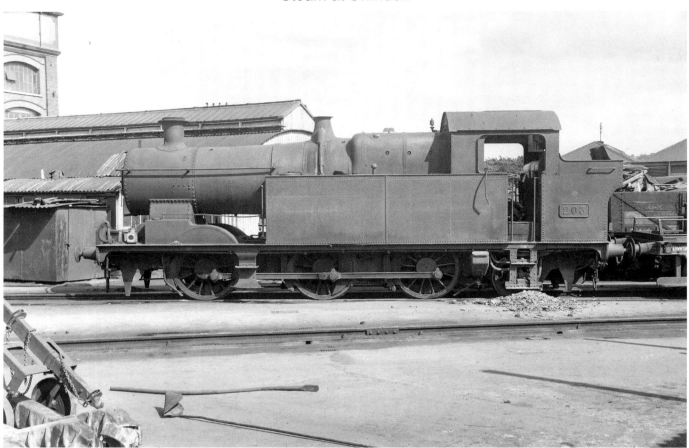

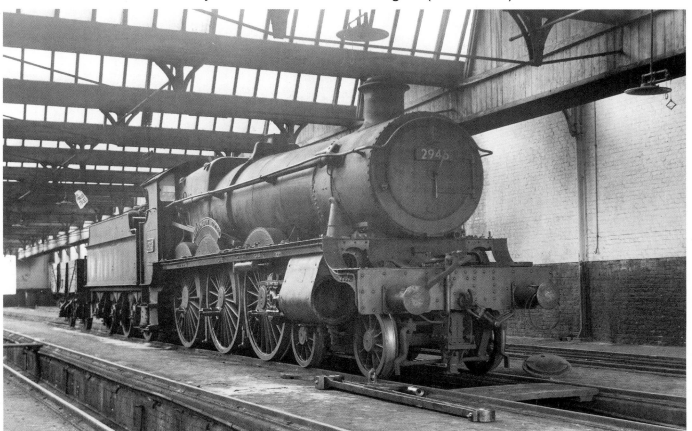

Opposite top: The Taff Vale Railway was the most profitable of the constituent companies that joined the Great Western in 1922 and 0-6-2T No 203 was one of forty-one O4 Class locomotives designed by Tom Hurry Riches for mixed traffic work. Built at the Vulcan Foundry Company (Newton-le-Willows) in September 1910 as TVR No 108, it was to be renumbered twice by the GWR, firstly as No 310 at the Grouping and again in December 1948 to the identity depicted here. The boiler is a superheated tapered Standard No 3 type, which it received at Swindon in September 1924 and the livery underneath the grime is plain black with the short-lived British Railways in Gill Sans font. The unusual domed and pitched roofed corrugated shed in the background accommodated the Works Pilot footplatemen and BSE workers who manned the nearby Reception Shed and 65ft turntable. Also present is the usual attendant wagon containing off-cuts of wood from the Carriage Shops, that were used in the lighting-up of ex-works locomotives prior to testing. 15 June 1952. *RCR 2199-3948 (915)*

Opposite bottom: Despite only being a matter of two weeks old, British Railways Standard Class 3 2-6-2T No 82007 is already showing the signs of workaday weathering as it graces Swindon shed yard on 15 June 1952. Designed by Robert Riddles, this forty-five strong class of 5'3" wheeled passenger tanks were all built in the adjacent Works between April 1952 and August 1955. Withdrawn from Bristol Barrow Road (82E) on 29 June 1964, it was cut at Cashmore's of Newport that December. Despite a similar fate befalling the entire class, at the time of writing a new-build example (No 82045) is taking shape in the Bridgnorth Workshops of the Severn Valley Railway. *RCR 2199-3948 (918)*

Above: Erected in 1886, the Stock Shed was intended to provide secure covered accommodation for locomotives awaiting entry into the Works for attention or short term storage for new and ex-works engines awaiting allocation or despatch to their respective running sheds. Inside the unusually empty six-road shed on 15 June 1952 rests Saint Class 4-6-0 No 2945 *Hillingdon Court*. Constructed in June 1912 and receiving its outside steam pipes in January 1938, it had been a resident at the nearby Running Shed prior to being placed into storage pending a final Light bottom-end overhaul in 'A' Shop, preparation for which appears to have already commenced. A short return to traffic at Cardiff Canton (86C) shed occurred on 1 November 1952, before withdrawal and scrapping back at Swindon on 30 June 1953. *RCR 2199-3948 (920)*

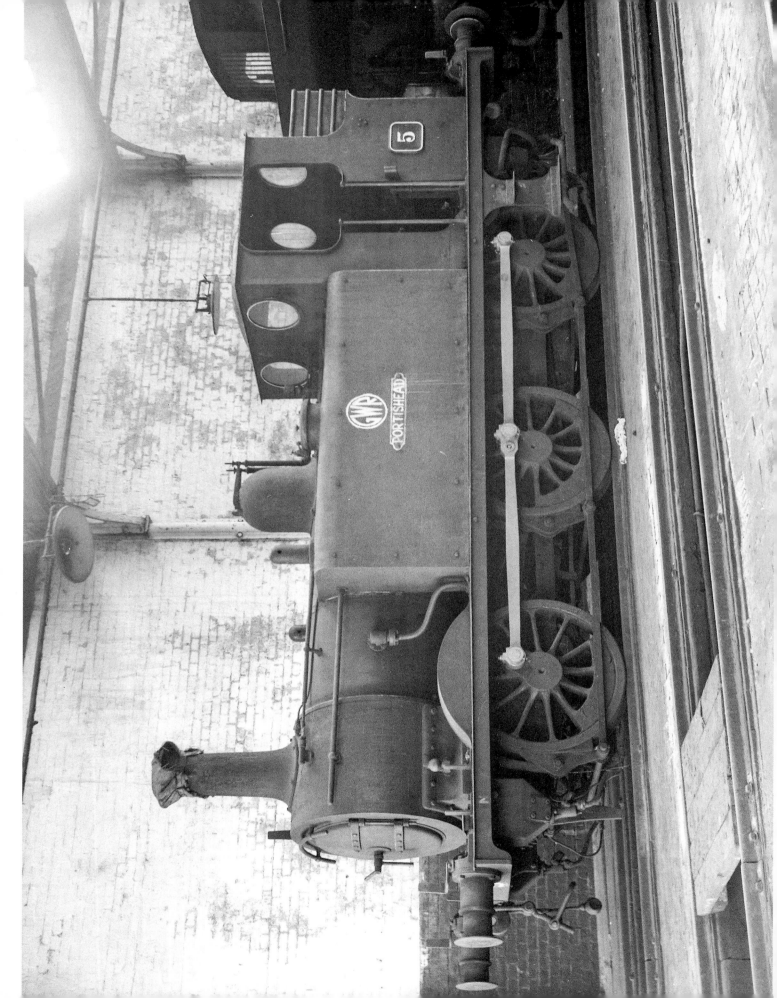

Opposite: Another gem stored within the Stock Shed on the same date was William Stroudley 'Terrier' A1X Class 0-6-0T No 5 *Portishead*, awaiting further use that was sadly never to come. Built at the Brighton Works of the London Brighton & South Coast Railway in June 1877 as No 43 *Gipsyhill*, it was to be one of a pair of the class sold to the Weston Clevedon & Portishead Light Railway in December 1925. Purchased for the princely sum of £785, the WC&PLR christened it No 2 *Portishead* within their eclectic fleet of locomotives, which were in turn acquired by the Great Western Railway upon closure of the line in May 1940. Renumbered by the GWR as No 5 but retaining the name, it was allocated to Bristol St Philips Marsh shed in 1941, initially working on the Bristol Harbour lines, Portishead Power Station and the Wapley Common US Army Depot. Later moves saw employment at the Taunton Concrete Works and a brief unsuccessful flirtation as the Newton Abbot Works Pilot before withdrawal January 1950. Upon return to Swindon it was placed within the Stock Shed, but perhaps due to its 'foreign' origin, did not muster enough interest for potential preservation and was scrapped in March 1954. *RCR 2199-3948 (921)*

Above: With the Swindon Works and Shed visit complete and the enthusiasts loaded back aboard their rake of carmine and cream ex-GWR Collett coaches, the SLS 'Saint Special' passes Swindon West Signal Box at the start of the return working to Birmingham. No 2920 *Saint David* was to put in a faultless performance, travelling via Didcot West Curve, Oxford, Banbury (with a stop to visit Banbury (84C) shed) and arriving back at Birmingham Snow Hill at 9:35pm.

Dick captured this image from the platform end at Swindon Station and it is a scene awash with the infrastructure associated with a working steam railway. Today most of the buildings are gone, the track layout hugely rationalised and the overhead lines, which once carried telegraph wires, are replaced by the 25kV catenary of the GW Main Line electrification scheme. *RCR 2199-3948 (923)*

Opposite: It is hard to believe that a mere $3^{1}/_{2}$ years separate the construction of the three locomotives captured in this photograph taken at the western end of Swindon Station on 12 January 1953. Castle Class 4-6-0 No 7024 *Powis Castle* approaching with an Up Paddington express was a June 1949 build and is only ten days back in traffic following a Heavy General overhaul. Riddles Britannia Class 4-6-2 No 70020 *Mercury* was built at Crewe in July 1951 and is awaiting the right of way with a Down Bristol express. In the background 94xx Class 0-6-0PT No 8430 is conducting Station Pilot duties as part of its running-in trials, having just been delivered new from W.G. Bagnall Ltd of Stafford. The Castle and Britannia were both residents of Old Oak Common (81A) shed whilst the 94xx was about to be allocated to Reading (81D). *RCR 2199-3948 (1072)*

Above: It is fair to say that when the first of the fifteen Riddles Standard Class 7 Britannia Pacifics (70015-70029) began to arrive on the Western Region from mid 1951, they were not received with great enthusiasm. Despite having been adorned with the names of former GWR Broad Gauge locomotives and the fitting of Western style lamp irons and ATC equipment, the fact that they were left-hand drive was central to their unpopularity with footplate crews. That and an unbreakable favour for their beloved Castles and Kings on the premier express turns. Despite their perceived shortcomings the 'Western Brits' were to give some sterling service, especially on South Wales diagrams, before their regular association with the region ceased in September 1961. The crew of No 70020 *Mercury* give Dick Riley their undivided attention from the confines of the warm cab on a cold foggy winter's morning, before lifting their express westwards on 12 January 1953. *RCR 2199-3948 (1073)*

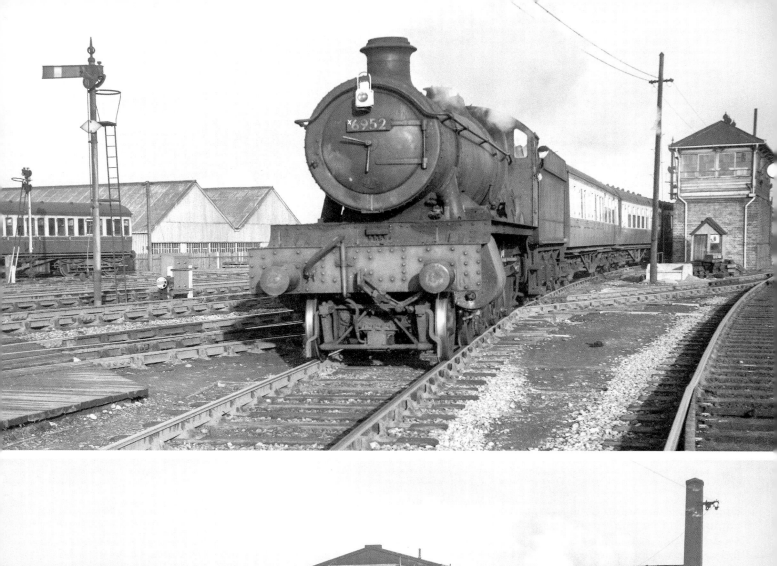

Opposite top: The time is almost 2.15pm on Monday 12 January 1953, if the clock on the side of Swindon East Signal Box is to be believed. Hall Class 4-6-0 No 6952 *Kimberley Hall* of Didcot (81E) shed arrives into Platform 1 (the down loop) with what is almost certainly the 1.15pm down stopping passenger working from Didcot, timetabled to arrive into Swindon at 2.14pm (so bang on time). After a layover, the train would form the return working to Didcot at 5.45pm. The filthy locomotive, typical condition for Didcot's allocation, was part of the final batch of Collett designed Halls entering service on 22 February 1943. Due to wartime measures, Nos 6916-6970 began life unnamed, featuring only the words *HALL CLASS* painted on the centre splasher, and it was not until September 1948 that No 6952 eventually received its plates. *Kimberley Hall* was an 18th century residence near Wymondham in Norfolk, whose name was one of several grand houses from outside of Great Western territory to adorn members of the Hall class.
The East Box was opened in 1911 and contained a 69-lever frame controlling that end of the Station approaches in addition to Station Road Sidings (on the right) and the Water Sidings, which usually contained coaching stock (as seen on the left). *RCR 2199-3948 (1076)*

Opposite bottom: *Swindon* of Swindon (82C) at Swindon! Waiting on an empty milk train in Platform 4 (down main) on 12 January 1953, the low afternoon winter sun illuminates the last of the hugely successful Castle Class 4-6-0s, No 7037 *Swindon*. Outshopped in August 1950 and originally earmarked for allocation to Worcester shed it was instead stored in the Stock Shed until 8 November 1950, when it was specially prepared for naming adorned with the Borough Coat of Arms beneath on the splasher.
The official ceremony was part of the Borough's Golden Jubilee celebrations and took place within the Works on 15 November 1950, unveiled by HRH Princess Elizabeth. The soon to become Queen had arrived in the Royal Train from Paddington, appropriately hauled by Star Class No 4057 *Princess Elizabeth*, which she famously drove from the Works back to the Station on the return journey to London. The locomotive, seen here attached to flat-sided Hawksworth (4000 gallon water, 6-ton coal capacity) tender No 4101, was to be withdrawn on 4 March 1963 and scrapped by Cashmore's of Newport by August 1965. Both nameplates and one of the special splashers do survive however, displayed in STEAM - Museum of the Great Western Railway within the former 'R' (Fitting & Machine) Shop. *RCR 2199-3948 (1078)*

Above: In the area colloquially known as 'The Triangle', situated in the vee of the diverging Bristol and Gloucester lines, was where all new admissions to the Works were initially deposited and held prior to being called forward to the Reception Shed. On a foggy 24 January 1953 the last of the King Class 4-6-0s No 6029 *King Edward VIII* waits its turn to be shunted along to the 'A' Shop end of the site. Note how the locomotive is completely as removed from traffic, steam pressure dropped but fully coaled and with the boiler still full of water. The Engine History card states that it arrived from its home shed of Plymouth Laira (83D) the previous day and was about to receive a Light Casual overhaul, which was completed on 5 March. Built in August 1930 as *King Stephen*, No 6029 was renamed on 14 May 1936 following the death of King George V and in recognition of the short reign of his eldest son Edward. In its original guise it was also selected to represent the GWR at the Liverpool & Manchester Railway Centenary Exhibition in September 1930. *RCR 2199-3948 (1092)*

Above: Looking in the opposite direction along the admission sidings to the previous image, Dick recorded Saint Class 4-6-0 No 2933 *Bibury Court* and Standard Class 2 2-6-0 No 78003 awaiting their summons to enter the Works. The Standard Mogul was one of a pair (the tender of 78002 can be seen on the left) that had just arrived fresh from build at Darlington and was entering Swindon to have ATC fitted prior to beginning work on the Western Region at Oswestry (89A). The Saint however, was to have already made its final journey in steam from its home shed at Leamington (84D). Note the storm sheet still in situ between the exposed Churchward cab and 3500g tender. One of only four class members to soldier on into 1953, *Bibury Court* was to be officially withdrawn within hours of this photograph being taken. Also visible is 51xx Class 2-6-2T No 5147, which is to suffer an identical fate to the Saint. 24 January 1953. *RCR 2199-3948 (1094)*

Opposite top: With the General and Drawing Offices looming large in the background, 2301 Class 'Dean Goods' 0-6-0 No 2462 sits sandwiched between No 6805 *Broughton Grange* and No 70019 *Lightning* on 24 January 1953. The venerable 0-6-0 had just arrived back at its December 1895 birthplace for scrapping, having worked out the final years of its 57-year life from St Philips Marsh shed in Bristol. The immediate area around the admission sidings was also locally referred to as 'The Pool', in reference to the fact that once locomotives had been left there, for accountancy purposes they officially became part of the 'Swindon Factory Pool' for the duration of their stay in the Works. *RCR 2199-3948 (1096)*

Opposite bottom: The five members of the 1361 Class 0-6-0ST were the last saddle tanks built at Swindon, in 1910. Although Churchward as the CME is credited, it was actually Swindon's Chief Draughtsman Harold Holcroft who designed these short 11'0" wheelbase engines for shunting in locations where the track radius was severe. Weighing just 35 tons and with 16" cylinders driving Allan outside valve gear, they produced a credible 14,835 lbs of tractive effort. On 24 January 1953, recently outshopped No 1365 stands amidst a tank engine cavalcade at the mouth of Swindon shed yard, awaiting despatch back to Plymouth Laira and a resumption of its duties in Millbay Docks and Sutton Harbour. *RCR 2199-3948 (1105)*

Throughout the 1950s a substantial amount of new construction work came the way of Swindon courtesy of the BR Standard designs, with 75000, 77000, 82000 and 92000 classes all built in 'A' Shop. In addition to this, the final batch of Ivatt Class 2 2-6-0s that were destined for service on the Western Region were outshopped under Lot 394. On 24 January 1953, No 46518 has emerged into the sunshine for the very first time, resplendent in its mixed traffic lined black livery. Side facing WR lamp irons are in evidence and other local refinements included a GWR-type vacuum ejector and firehole door. Interestingly the builders plate states 'BUILT 1952 SWINDON', the date relating to when the frames were laid down rather than when the locomotive was completed. Twenty-two of the Swindon 'Mickey Mouse' moguls including this one, went initially to Oswestry shed for work on the Cambrian, with the final three going to Bristol St Philips Marsh. *RCR 2199-3948 (1099)*

Dick Riley himself stated that his photography really began to improve from 1954 onwards, aided in no small part by him joining the Maurice Earley Railway Photographic Society which amongst other things encouraged his own developing and printing. Another contributory factor was his purchase of an Agfa Isolette camera in 1955, which featured a built in viewfinder, 1/500-second capable shutter and exposed 2¼ inch square negatives. This new square format is clearly evident in the next couple of images of Star Class 4-6-0 No 4061 *Glastonbury Abbey* alongside No 5030 *Shirburn Castle* undergoing overhauls in 'A' Shop on 13 May 1955. *R5001-6100 (1072)*

These wonderful images demonstrate the labour intensive nature of the work undertaken in each of the maintenance bays, with teams of different tradesmen attending to locomotives in the rotational cycle of its shopping. Here No 4061 *Glastonbury Abbey* nears the end of a Heavy Intermediate, with cab refitting the apparent focus of attention. Amongst the clutter on the floor, items such as the cab fallplate and huge single chimney, which will require lifting into position by one of the overhead cranes, await a return to their rightful place. As can be seen, it was GWR practice to repaint locomotives in situ, rather than have a dedicated Paint Shop, as at works such as Crewe and Doncaster. *Glastonbury Abbey* was destined to be the penultimate Star in traffic, being withdrawn on 11 March 1957 from Wolverhampton Stafford Road (84A). 13 May 1955. *R5001-6100 (1074)*

Top: Kerr Stuart 0-6-0T No 666 was part of a consignment of ten locomotives built in 1917 for Government use, before purchase in November 1919 by the Alexandra (Newport & South Wales) Docks and Railway. It was withdrawn from Newport Pill (86B) shed during April 1955 and by the time of this photograph on 13 May, had reached Swindon and already lost its centre wheelset and motion. Above the cab is a BR(W) design tubular post Siding Outlet Signal with 3ft arm and 'Cash Register' type Route Indicator featuring what appear to be five alternative slides. This signal controlled movement from the lines alongside 'A' Shop and the Weighbridge House towards the Reception Shed and the Up goods loop. *R5001-6100 (1076)*

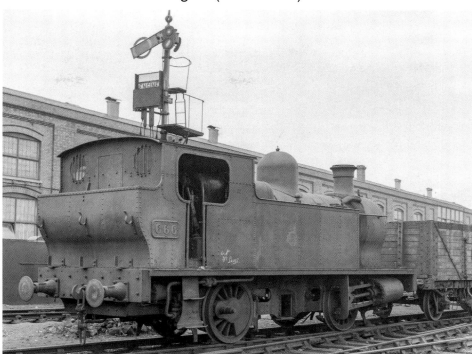

Bottom: Hawksworth County Class 4-6-0 No 1020 *County of Monmouth* occupies one of the spur sidings off the turntable on 13 May 1955. It looks to be receiving some last minute attention to its left hand piston valve prior to being released back to Neyland (87H) shed in Pembrokeshire, West Wales. The 'Counties' were the final evolution of the Great Western 4-6-0 family, built between 1945-47 and were to feature a number of design deviations. Plate frames supported an all-new Standard No 15 boiler constructed from nickel steel alloy and pressured to 280lbs psi, and the driving wheels at 6'3" were also a new size for Swindon. The full width cab and tender at 8'6" was another Hawksworth initiative unique to this class of thirty locomotives and whilst another thirty-five were planned, these were to be cancelled, replaced by further batches of Modified Halls and Castles. *R5001-6100 (1077)*

Opposite top: On 13 May 1955, with the spire of St Mark's Church piercing the skyline, Castle Class 4-6-0 No 5083 *Bath Abbey* passes the Works at the head of the Down 1.18pm Paddington to Bristol Temple Meads service. It has been fitted with a reporting frame, but no numerals, for this short five-coach formation and despite the illusion the vans and wagons to the rear are in fact stabled on the sidings alongside the Saw Mill and No.4 Carriage Shop! Rebuilt in June 1937 from Star Class No 4063, *Bath Abbey* had recently emerged from a Heavy Intermediate where it acquired the 4000g Hawksworth tender No 4097. One of five Castles converted to oil burning between December 1946 and November 1948 (a legacy from which are the cab roof shutters), it was also destined to be one of the first of the class to be withdrawn, on 7 January 1959. *R5001-6100 (1078)*

Opposite bottom: On a bright spring morning, Collett Hall Class 4-6-0 No 5983 *Henley Hall* gets the right away from Platform 1, past Swindon West Signal Box at the head of the 7.35am down slow to Bristol on 14 May 1955. As was not uncommon amongst the Halls during the early 1950s, the locomotive carries mixed traffic lined black but is paired with a plain green tender still bearing the G (Crest) W branding. This does however appear to be well stocked with good lumps of the finest Welsh steam coal. *R5001-6100 (1079)*

Above: After a quick dash to the other end of Swindon Station, Dick was able to capture County Class 4-6-0 No 1014 *County of Glamorgan* entering Platform 4 from the east, with a down 'Class C' express parcels train. First entering traffic on 18 February 1946, it was one of the initial nineteen locomotives to run unnamed, eventually fitted with the unique straight plates in March 1948. A long time Bristol Bath Road (82A) resident, it here still retains the original single chimney, which was to be replaced with the rather squat looking double version in May 1958. The distinctive Hawksworth flat-sided 4000g tender (in this case No 129) was from a batch only compatible with the Counties, as similar vehicles used behind Castles and Halls were some six inches narrower. Alongside, No 4971 *Stanway Hall* of Taunton (83B) shed is passing on the up through road. *R5001-6100 (1080)*

Opposite top: Looking south towards the distant Newburn Carriage Shed we find 'Simplex' shunter No 26 in the Sawmills Yard, adjacent to the (AW) Wheel Shop outside Travelling Crane (just out of shot to the left). Powered by a 4-cylinder petrol engine, it was the last of five purchased and delivered to the GWR in April 1927, destined for use at the Didcot Provender Stores. It had however been back working at Swindon from at least early 1954, employed at various locations around the Works including within 'B' Shop and the western end yards. The chimneys seen in the foreground were typical of the relics to be discovered littering this area of the site. 12 September 1955. *RCR 6101-7100 (472)*

Opposite Bottom: Hurry Riches designed Rhymney Railway R Class 0-6-2T No 39 forms a line of newly condemned locomotives outside 'A' Shop on 12 September 1955. Constructed by Beyer Peacock Ltd in December 1921 as RR No 43, the GWR renumbered it to No 39 at the Grouping and subsequently rebuilt it with a tapered boiler in May 1930. The commonplace substantial patch weld repair to the lower tank side is also clearly visible. It had been withdrawn from Cardiff East Dock (88B) three weeks previously and following storage in the Conyard was scrapped in mid December. *RCR 6101-7100 (474)*

Above: The larger version of the Wolverhampton built six-coupled saddle tanks were the Dean 2021 Class, which as per common practice were to be rebuilt as panniers. October 1899 built No 2070 received this treatment in May 1926, when it also gained an enclosed cab and enlarged bunker. Its livery here at withdrawal is still the final style of GWR green but of note are the non-standard red painted cabside number and London Midland Region style smokebox numberplate which are a result of an overhaul received at Crewe Works during 1950. It had accumulated just short of 56 years service, lately at Bristol St Philips Marsh and only has the final short journey to 'C' Shop to come. 12 September 1955. *RCR 6101-7100 (476)*

Above: Isolated amongst condemned wagons in the Conyard sidings, Dick discovered another recently withdrawn ex-Rhymney Railway 0-6-2T in the shape of AP Class No 78. The four members of the AP Class were built by Hudswell Clarke and Company Limited of Leeds, and were delivered just before the Grouping in August 1921. They were intended for main line passenger working between Cardiff and Rhymney, as evidenced by the provision of a steam heating pipe. No 78 received a Standard No 10 boiler as late as November 1949, giving it the distinction of being the last absorbed locomotive to be rebuilt by the BR(W). One can only speculate however as to the meaning behind the 'Junky Chunky' embellishment to the smokebox door! *RCR 6101-7100 (478)*

Opposite top: Castle Class 4-6-0 No 5050 *Earl of St Germans* of Shrewsbury (84G) shed on a short six-coach formation consisting of ex-LNER stock, heading west past the south-side Carriage Shops on 12 September 1955. It is thought the train is the 12.20pm York to Swansea service that ran via the Great Central route to Banbury and was scheduled to call at Swindon between 6.00-6.07pm. The locomotive was recently released from a Heavy General where it received the brand new four-row superheated boiler No 7658, and has possibly taken over the train as a running-in turn. For some reason the 'Earls' did not receive the additional 'CASTLE CLASS' wording below the name, found on the aircraft, abbey and personage renames. *RCR 6101-7100 (480)*

Opposite bottom: The construction of Castle class locomotives recommenced after WW2, with a further forty examples built in three batches between 1946-50. They were easily distinguished from the earlier builds by a revised handrail curving around the cabside window and No 7015 *Carn Brea Castle* was from the middle Lot. 367 released to traffic in July 1948. Here it stands amongst 3' and 3' 2" bogie wheels alongside 'The Barn' on 12 September 1955, having been in 'A' Shop since 12 August receiving a Heavy General overhaul. Double chimneys were yet to be fitted to the Castles and the mechanical lubricator remains in the original position behind the steampipe on the running plate. The loose bogie immediately behind the open wagon has a plate or label hanging down identifying which engine it belongs to, believed to read '5037'. The real Carn Brea Castle is actually an 18th century stone folly, built to represent a medieval castle and is located near Redruth in Cornwall. The Grade II structure today functions as a restaurant. *RCR 6101-7100 (487)*

Opposite top: On Monday 12 September 1955, members of the Stephenson Locomotive Society absorb the sights and sounds of Swindon shed yard. Old Oak Common's No 5940 *Whitbourne Hall* (still wearing a Down ex-Paddington train reporting number) appears to have been serviced and turned ready for an imminent return to London. To the rear can be seen the elevated coal wagon road and the roof profiles of the nine-road straight running shed of 1871, and higher pitched 1908 'roundhouse' extension shed to the right. *RCR 6101-7100 (481)*

Opposite bottom: Obscured by the Hall in the previous image, recently ex-works duo No 7028 *Cadbury Castle* of Landore (87E) and 6015 *King Richard III* of Old Oak Common (81A) stand on No.8 Road awaiting despatch back to their parent sheds. Both engines had undergone a Heavy General with the King spending an extended 73 days in 'A' Shop receiving new front frames, inside cylinders and most noticeably an experimental fabricated double chimney. Following successful trials, this new blastpipe arrangement was introduced to the whole class, although the final design of chimney adopted had a much more pleasing elliptical profile. 12 September 1955. *RCR 6101-7100 (482)*

Above: Within the confines of their home shed building at Swindon (82A), Castle Class 4-6-0 No 5083 *Bath Abbey* stands in the company of Standard Class 4 4-6-0 No 75002 and 56xx Class 0-6-2T No 6699 on 18 September 1955. The locomotives are stabled around the 65ft turntable situated in the 1908 extension, with the opening through to the earlier straight shed marked by the Collett tender standing at right angles in the background. One of the original wooden smoke hoods remains above the cab of the Castle, whilst most of the others appear to have been replaced by newer metal alternatives. Dick would have almost certainly made use of a tripod to capture this image inside the gloomy shed environs. *RCR 6101-7100 (535)*

Above: Back outside the front of the straight shed occupying No.6 Road, we find Castle No 5060 *Earl of Berkeley*. With apparent steam to spare and well-coaled ready for a return working to London, its unkempt external condition is typical of Old Oak Common locomotives and would have incurred the wrath of Shedmasters at the likes of Landore, Newton Abbot and Worcester. Still fitted with a two-row superheated boiler, it also carries the shorter version of the Castle single chimney introduced on engines built from 1936. No.5 Road alongside the locomotive was always left clear, in order to allow unrestricted access to the 45ft turntable at the rear of the original shed building. 18 September 1955. *RCR 6101-7100 (537)*

Opposite top: An immaculate Collett 56xx Class 0-6-2T No 6654 stands on the busy turntable spur sidings between the Boiler De-Tubing House and the Pattern Store on 18 September 1955. The eclectic company includes ex-Taff Vale O4 Class 0-6-2T No 215, 57xx 0-6-0PT No 8738 and ex-Cardiff Railway Hudswell Clarke 0-6-0PT No 681. The 56xx is a member of the final batch of fifty locomotives built under licence by Armstrong Whitworth & Co Ltd in August 1928, and was one of a pair allocated to Southall (81C) for freight workings along the Thames Valley. To the left a fascinating collection of steam domes are congregating outside 'The Barn', and note also the alignment locking-bar situated within the shallow turntable pit. *RCR 6101-7100 (539)*

Opposite bottom: Frederick Hawksworth's tenure as CME (1941-1949) saw him responsible for the introduction of the 15xx, 16xx and 94xx classes of 0-6-0PT, but it is probably for his two 4-6-0 designs, the Modified Halls and Counties, that he is best remembered. Undoubtedly the 6959 Class or 'Modified Hall' was the most successful of these, with Hawksworth incorporating a series of improvements into the original Collett design of 1924. On 18 September 1955, No 6997 *Bryn-Ivor Hall*, a January 1949 build, shows off some of those modifications in its extruding plate frames, smokebox saddle, longer steampipes and revised cylinders. The canopy erected on to the end of the Boiler De-Tubing House was to provide some protection from the elements for workers tasked with rebuilding the firebox brick arches in newly overhauled locomotives. Some of these specialised bricks can just be discerned stacked under the awning. *RCR 6101-7100 (540)*

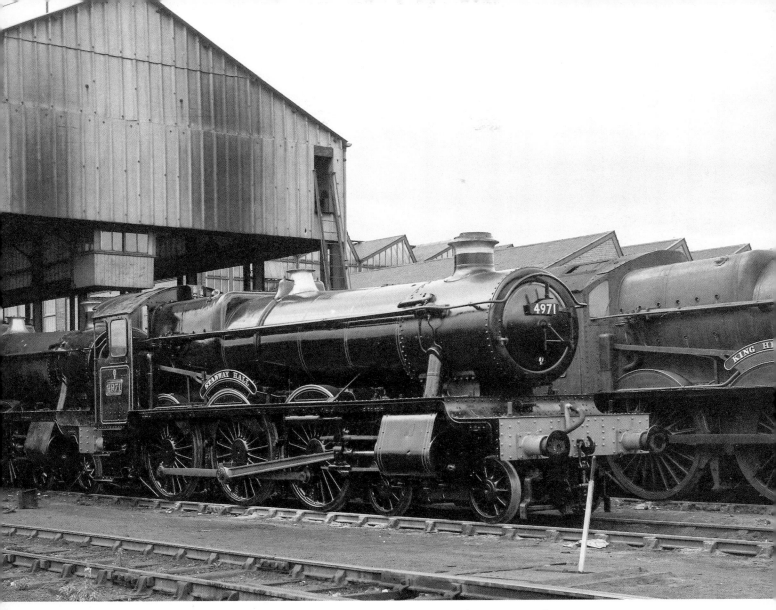

Opposite: Churchward 44xx Class 2-6-2T No 4410 was the last of the eleven 4' 1¹/₂" wheeled Small Prairies built at Wolverhampton in June 1906. Released to service as No 3110, it was an early renumber to 4410 in December 1912 and spent its entire working life in the southwest, latterly on the Princetown Branch from Plymouth Laira (83D). It was the only member of the class not to have a 9" extension added to the rear frames to facilitate an enlarged bunker, and as such the numberplate only just squeezed into position! It was as a result of a heavy shunting incident causing the visible drooping of the rear footplate, in addition to the imminent closure of the Princetown Branch, that sealed its withdrawal on 12 September 1955. Having accumulated a respectable 993,193 miles, it finally succumbed to the cutter's torch on 8 October. 18 September 1955. *RCR 6101-7100 (542)*

Above: Collett Hall Class 4-6-0 No 4971 *Stanway Hall* of Taunton (83B) shed stands freshly shopped outside the Reception Shed, awaiting the arrival of a suitable tender from 'B' Shop. One of eleven Halls selected for conversion to burn fuel oil as a result of post-war austerity measures, *Stanway Hall* was temporarily renumbered No 3901 between May 1947 and April 1949 as a means of distinguishing from unaltered class members. Alongside the Hall is No 6014 *King Henry VII*, instantly recognisable from the wedge-fronted cab, a legacy of its ill-fated streamlining experiment of 1935. The 1944 built Reception Shed was specifically provided as covered accommodation to prepare locomotives for entry into the Shops, including separation from their tender (if applicable), removal of coal and ash, water drained from tanks and boilers and firebox brick arches dropped. This process would be repeated in reverse to make ready for testing, on completion of their overhaul. 18 September 1955. *RCR 6101-7100 (541)*

Above: A view for which Swindon Works is perhaps most instantly recognised; resplendent steam locomotives just released from the confines of 'A' Shop. Captured on 18 September 1955, Churchward 43xx Class 2-6-0 No 5380 heads Collett Hall Class 4-6-0's No 5988 *Bostock Hall* and No 4912 *Berrington Hall* as they await the 'A' Shop Pilot to move them to the Reception Shed and allocation of tenders. This was one of several compositions from 1955 onwards that Dick replicated on both Black and White and Colour film. *RCR 6101-7100 (543)*

Opposite top: Some photographs in every collection can throw up more questions than answers and this is one such example. The date is Sunday 18 September 1955 and Newton Abbot (83A) based Castle No 5079 *Lysander* passes between 'A' Shop and Rodbourne Lane Signal Box, with what Dick Riley simply annotated as a Wolverhampton to Penzance train. The premier express between those locations was 'The Cornishman' and the lengthy formation of BR Mk1 and ex-GWR coaches adorned with carriage boards resembles such a set. The regular route for the train however was via Stratford and Gloucester to Bristol, and a possible reason for its presence at Swindon was down to a diversion via Oxford due to weekend engineering works. The usual engine change from a Stafford Road to a Newton Abbot Castle could therefore have taken place at Oxford or Swindon rather than Bristol Temple Meads. The author would be pleased to hear of any alternative theories or evidence to solve the mystery. *RCR 6101-7100 (546)*

Opposite bottom: Two fine candidates for preservation in the shape of former Cardiff Railway Hudswell Clarke 0-6-0PT No 683 and ex-Taff Vale O4 Class 0-6-2T No 205 occupy the headshunt to the east of the Rodbourne Road bridge. The Cardiff Railway was the smallest of the constituent companies absorbed by the Great Western in 1922 and most of its locomotives were either sold or scrapped not long after Grouping. No 683 was one of four identical saddle tanks built in 1920, and followed the time honoured conversion to pannier configuration at Swindon in October 1926. Sadly any thoughts of saving such workaday examples of our industrial heritage were outside the aspirations of the fledgling railway preservation movement. 18 September 1955. *RCR 6101-7100 (550)*

Interesting treasures were to be discovered around every corner within the Swindon Works site, as typified by this classic Riley cameo of a collection of cast iron chimneys taken on 18 September 1955. The two fitted with the iconic Great Western copper caps are identified as belonging to 56xx Class No 5614 and County Class No 1010 *County of Caernarvon*. *RCR 6101-7100 (551)*

Sandwiched between Collett 2884 Class 2-8-0s Nos 3837 and 3839 on No.9 Road of Swindon shed on 16 June 1957, sits Churchward 43xx Class 2-6-0 No 4358. Belonging to Gloucester (85B) shed, the mogul wears fully lined BR green including the tender side fender, complete with the early 'cycling lion' emblem of 1949. Having received a relatively recent overhaul at Caerphilly Works, the April 1914 built locomotive was destined to be the last of the 43xx numbered examples, remaining in service until August 1959. Directly behind the engine is the Running Shed Main Office building, containing the Shedmaster's Office and Accounts Office, where an addressograph machine printed all the wage paybills for footplate and shed staff. *RCR 10801 (2)*

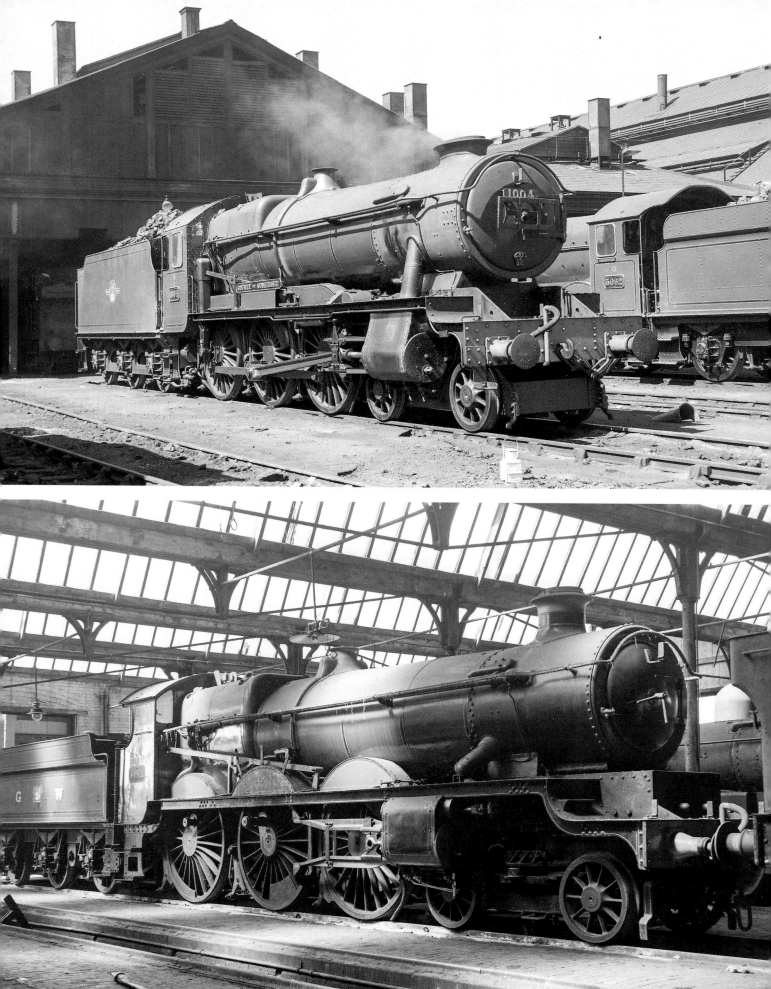

Opposite top: Just to the left of the view on the previous page, a favourite position for Dick to capture three-quarter locomotive portraits, are resident Hawksworth County Class 4-6-0 No 1004 *County of Somerset* and Castle Class No 5062 *Earl of Shaftesbury*. As indicated by their external condition, both engines are fresh from recent overhauls and carry the latest British Railways heraldic crest, introduced in March 1957 and often referred to as the 'ferret and dartboard'. The County as part of its Heavy General has acquired a double chimney and self-cleaning smokebox apparatus, indicated by the 'SC' below the 82C shedplate. *RCR 10801 (3)*

Opposite bottom: As described on page 38, the restoration of Star Class 4-6-0 No 4003 *Lode Star* was to be a protracted affair taking over ten years. During much of that time it was placed into storage within the Stock Shed, as it is seen here on 16 June 1957. Built in February 1907 at a cost of £3,180, it was to carry seventeen different boilers during its 44-year service history, amassing a grand total of 2,005,898 miles run. Cited by many as one of the finest of all Great Western Railway locomotive designs, the preservation of a Churchward Star was considered essential and it has been a central exhibit at both Swindon and the National Railway Museum in York. *RCR 10801 (4)*

Above: Sunday 25 August 1957 saw Dick tour the Swindon site as part of a regular public opening. Against a backdrop of newly arrived tenders destined for attention in 'B' Shop, he was rewarded with a sparkling ex-works Churchward 42xx Class 2-8-0T No 4255. These very powerful heavy freight tanks were rated E Red by the GWR (over 33,000lb of tractive effort and axle weight above 17tons 12cwt), which equated to BR 7F, and came in at an all up weight of 82 tons. Built in April 1917, this locomotive was fitted with outside steam pipes in October 1945 but retained the original square drop-end running plate. An Aberdare (86J) engine at the time of the photograph, it was certain not to remain in this pristine condition for long. *RCR 10801 (354)*

Above: Waiting to be collected from 'The Pool' for assessment and a decision to be made on its future, is Collett 54xx Class 0-6-0PT No 5403 of Westbury (82D) shed. The news was not to be positive, as it was officially condemned two days later and hastily scrapped within a month. Still wearing wartime GWR black, this large 5' 2" wheeled pannier was from a class of twenty-five designed for passenger work, and was built at Swindon in December 1931. The boiler was a Standard No 21 and just visible is the top feed that was added during 1945. All engines were auto-fitted and featured a screw reverser, which was more conducive to passenger operations. Across the main running lines can be seen the doors to No 8 Carriage Paint Shop and the outside traverser used for moving vehicles around the bays and from the adjacent No 7 Carriage Finishing Shop. 25 August 1957. *RCR 10801 (360)*

Opposite top: A typically grubby Old Oak Common King Class 4-6-0 No 6007 *King William III* rests at Swindon shed on 25 August 1957. This was the locomotive involved in a serious accident at Shrivenham on 15 January 1936 and, despite being officially withdrawn due to the damage sustained, it was actually rebuilt using the same frames and boiler and returned to service. Due to the intensive nature of their work hauling the heaviest trains, by the mid-1950s many Kings were exhibiting weakened and cracked frames which resulted in a programme of remedial work at Swindon. Here No 6007 shows evidence of that work, having received new front frames and an inside cylinder block during a lengthy Heavy General between April and September 1956. Externally this could be identified by revised covers to the inside valve spindles and the welding of circular strengthening plates to the front lifting holes. Also received during the same overhaul was this initial pattern of fabricated double chimney, which the first dozen modified locomotives received prior to November 1956; after this date a much more aesthetically pleasing cast iron second type was introduced (compare with image of No 6016 on page 79). *RCR 10801 (364)*

Opposite bottom: The pioneer of the non-auto fitted Collett 58xx Class 0-4-2T No 5800 is stabled at its home shed at Swindon on 25 August 1957. Both tank engines in this view are displaying the common aftermath of inaccurate use of the manual coaling tubs, resulting in overspill on to the cab roof. Emerging new from Swindon Works in January 1933, the locomotive spent its entire life working from 82C, apart from an initial short allocation to St Philips Marsh shed. Probably the most notable event of its career was hauling the last public passenger train on the Highworth Branch on Saturday 28 February 1953. It would eventually be withdrawn from service on 22 July 1958. *RCR 10801 (366)*

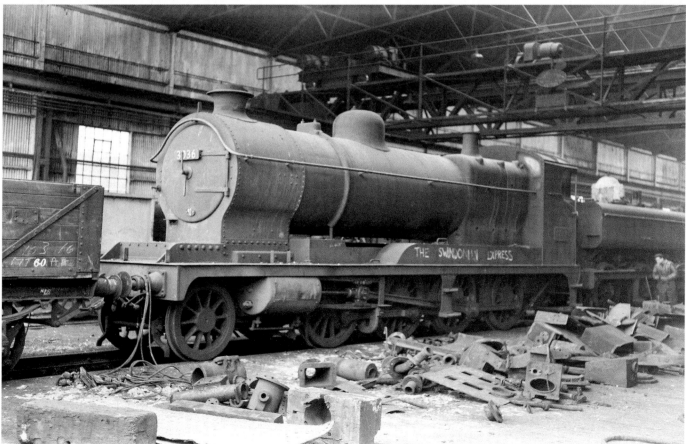

Opposite top: Having stood isolated in the Conyard for a number of months since withdrawal, Collett 57xx Class 0-6-0PTs Nos 5710 and 5741 await their turn for scrapping on 15 March 1958. Both of these early 1929 built locomotives were from the initial batch of fifty delivered by the North British Locomotive Company of Glasgow, and were subsequently amongst the first members of the class removed from service. Notice how on both engines the process of pouring coal into the bunkers has damaged the rear lip of the cab roof. *RCR 10801 (747)*

Opposite bottom: Probably due to exposure issues, Dick didn't attempt many photographs within the confines of the 'C' Shop building itself, so this one of ex-ROD 30xx Class 2-8-0 No 3036 formerly of Carmarthen (87G) is somewhat of a rarity. The large open-ended steel frame structure, clad in corrugated sheeting, was opened in 1929 and was equipped with an overhead crane (seen above the locomotive) with electro-magnetic grabber. Further large 10-ton goliath cranes served the outside sidings surrounding the shop, where it was also commonplace for cutting to take place when capacity inside was exceeded. It would be nice to think that the Swindonian Express adornment was applied by its former shed before the final journey from southwest Wales for scrapping. 15 March 1958. *RCR 10801 (750)*

Above: Alongside the main 'C' Shop building on the same date as the previous image, the cutter gets to work on the cab roof of 54xx Class 0-6-0PT No 5419. Withdrawn only three weeks previously from Westbury shed, there was no apparent reason why some locomotives spent months stored on the Conyard sidings whilst others were dispatched within a matter of days of arrival. Very conspicuous on the running plate are a pair of lubricating oil reservoirs, fitted to all 54xx and some 64xx panniers. The 54xx class like the 45xx next to it were victims of the onset of dieselisation and closure of some of the branch lines they operated. Behind the duo is a Diagram N22 20-ton Loco Coal wagon, possibly providing fuel to the boiler house beyond. *RCR 10801 (748)*

Opposite: With the cessation of small locomotive overhauls in 'B' Shop from 1956, all work was carried out exclusively within 'A' Shop. Here looking south in the original 1901 section of the shop, 1361 Class 0-6-0ST No 1361 is receiving the final touches to what was to be its last Heavy General overhaul on 15 March 1958. Whilst not as high as the 1920 extension, this part of 'A' Shop was still well lit and airy thanks to its saw-tooth north light roofing, covering eighty pit roads served by two traversers and 50-ton overhead cranes. The small dock tank was to go on to operate from Taunton (83B), Plymouth Laira (83D) and Weymouth (71G) sheds before eventual withdrawal in May 1961. *RCR 10801 (751)*

Above: 8750 Class 0-6-0PT No 3671 of Yeovil shed looks as shiny as a new penny as it awaits a steam test run by the turntable on 15 March 1958. The 4' 7½" wheeled 57xx and 8750 variant pannier tanks were the most numerous class of steam locomotives on the GWR, with 863 built between 1929-1950. Of this figure, 613 were constructed at Swindon with the remainder from outside contractors; Armstrong Whitworth (25), Beyer Peacock (25), Kerr Stuart (25), North British (100), W.G. Bagnall (50) and the Yorkshire Engine Company (25). This low angle highlights a wealth of detail for the modeller, including the closed position of the cab side shutter, usually slid away from view. *RCR 10801 (742)*

Opposite top: You could be forgiven for thinking Dick Riley had a soft spot for the absorbed South Wales tanks, as he certainly exposed a few rolls worth of film on them over the years. Taff Vale Railway A Class 0-6-2T No 373 awaits the official inspection that will confirm its final withdrawal and subsequent scrapping after a period as works pilot. Designed by John Cameron and eventually numbering fifty-eight, they formed the TVR's largest class of tank engines and this example was built in April 1919 by Nasmyth Wilson & Company Limited of Patricroft, Manchester. No 6708 was from a sub-class of fifty 57xx panniers (6700-49) built exclusively for shunting work, without steam heat, vacuum brakes or ATC and only fitted with 3-link couplings. 15 March 1958. *RCR 10801 (752)*

Opposite bottom: On 15 March 1958, 850 Class 0-6-0PT No 2008 has arrived at Swindon for scrapping from Birkenhead (6C) shed. Built as a saddle tank at Wolverhampton in November 1892 (see classmate No 2007 on page 28), it was converted into pannier form in June 1922 and was to be the penultimate member of the class in traffic, operating on the Birkenhead Docks system. Pictured here at 'The Triangle' in the company of Swindon shed's BR Standard Class 5 4-6-0 No 73018, this little tank engine retained its open cab to the end and had given a remarkable 65 years and 4 months service to the Great Western Railway, British Railways Western and latterly London Midland Regions. *RCR 10801 (754)*

Above: No 6016 *King Edward V* and No 5909 *Newton Hall* stand on shed ready for their next turns. The King was another example to receive new front frames and inside cylinders, on this occasion during late 1954. It has however been fitted with the second type of double chimney during a recent Heavy General, the style that was eventually to adorn all thirty locomotives. The Hall was a Worcester (85A) engine at this time and its ATC shoe apparatus is clearly visible hanging beneath the front coupling hook. Notice also the taller original chimney, as compared to the shorter slightly wider later version on the classmate to the left. As with many such details there is no hard and fast rule as to which type was carried on which locomotive, as numerous boiler changes only added to the mire of confusion. 15 March 1958. *RCR 10801 (756)*

Above: It may appear heresy to include photographs of diesel locomotives in a book entitled *Steam at Swindon*, but as mentioned in the introduction, Dick Riley took great steps to record the full diversity of what he encountered. On the same day and adjacent to the previous image, he photographed D6xx Warship Class No D600 *Active*, recently delivered from the North British Locomotive Company in Glasgow. The diesel hydraulic was still engaged in assessed trial runs and driver training and had only three weeks previously disgraced itself with an engine failure on the home leg of a Paddington to Bristol and return VIP special. Indeed it was to be 16 June 1958 before the class was deemed sufficiently reliable to regularly haul the non-stop Down 'Cornish Riviera' as far as Plymouth, in place of the established King. It is fair to conclude that the five members of the D6xx class were not an outstanding success and they were withdrawn en mass from Laira shed on New Year's Eve 1967. *RCR 10801 (757)*

Opposite top: On 26 April 1959 No 6985 *Parwick Hall* (85B) pulls to a stop at Swindon with the 9.15am Cheltenham-Paddington which it has worked from Gloucester. This and the following image record the long lost sequence of an engine changeover, a process that was once common practice across the railway network and occurred numerous times daily at Swindon alone. The oncoming Castle Class locomotive can be seen waiting in the Highworth Bay Platform (No.7) to the right. The train is made up of carmine and cream BR Mk1 coaches with a solitary maroon example next to a similarly liveried ex-GWR Churchward 12-wheel H15 Restaurant Car. Also notice how the main running lines have been re-laid with flatbottom rail, with the exception of the up through road that retains the original bullhead type. *RCR 12901-13999 (317)*

Opposite bottom: With the Hall now removed and having drawn forward out of the way, Castle Class No 5066 *Sir Felix Pole* (81A) has been released from the bay and backs down to take over the train for the remaining journey to London Paddington. Having just completed a Heavy General where it received a new four-row superheated boiler and a double chimney, the Castle had been undertaking running in turns for the previous four days and it is probable that this working was finally returning it to Old Oak Common. Originally *Wardour Castle*, it was renamed in April 1956 to honour the man who held the office of Great Western Railway General Manager between 1921 and 1929. Interesting rolling stock abounds in the background, including an ENPARTS branded MINK D (used for transporting locomotive spares from Swindon Works to running sheds) and a DD4 CORDON Gas Tank wagon. *RCR 12901-13999 (319)*

Opposite top: Southall allocated 61xx Large Prairie Class 2-6-2T No 6157 approaches Swindon from the east past the Cocklebury Sidings, with an engineer's train containing a Great Western Standard 6-Ton Steam Crane. The GWR built twenty-one of these cranes in-house to its own design between 1898 and 1923, and a considerable number were allocated to Swindon, working for the Loco, Traffic and Engineers Departments. Swindon Town Gasworks is seen in the distance, which was worked by the No.4 Pilot Link (Highworth Junction Up Side), delivering loaded coal wagons into the site and removing coke in return. 26 April 1959. *RCR 12901-13999 (321)*

Opposite bottom: Old Oak Common's No 6920 *Barningham Hall* slows for the Swindon stop on a down express on 26 April 1959. Although Dick made no record at the time, the train is thought to be the 9.05am Paddington-Weston super Mare due to call at 11.00am, and comprises of BR Mk1 coaches with an ex-GWR Collett D127 Brake Third interloper as the fourth vehicle. Lined maroon livery had been selected for mainline passenger coaches from May 1956 to replace the badly wearing carmine and cream, but the Western Region in its constant pursuit of individualism also reintroduced a variation of the iconic chocolate and cream for its premier express formations. The result was that for a large period of the late 1950s mixed rakes of coaches presented anything but the intended uniformity desired by the British Transport Commission. *RCR 12901-13999 (322)*

Above: Resident Collett 8750 Class 0-6-0PT No 9605 is engaged in a light shunting manoeuvre on to the Down through road (as indicated by the 1931 RCH pattern calling-on signal bottom right of the gantry) adjacent to Swindon East Signal Box on the late morning of 26 April 1959. East Box received the substantial brick re-enforcement skirt around its base during WW2, as a measure to protect it from potential bomb blast. To the right can be seen a new wooden Type 37 Signal Box to a design introduced from 1957. This 107-lever structure was intended to replace the existing East Box but was never commissioned, instead being relocated to Radyr Junction where it opened on 4 June 1961. The reason was that Swindon had been earmarked for a new Panel Room which was installed on the Down platform in 1968, commensurate with the advent of the multiple-aspect colour light signalling system (MAS). *RCR 12901-13999 (324)*

Opposite top: Amongst a batch of new arrivals to the admission sidings at 'The Triangle' on 26 April 1959 is Collett 74xx Class 0-6-0PT No 7415. The fifty 74xx lightweight panniers were truly maids of all work, and whilst non auto-fitted and equipped with a lever reverser (preferred for shunting), they were equally at home on branch passenger, yard shunting or station pilot duties all across the network. No 7415 had been built to Lot.307 in December 1936 and despite being withdrawn in February 1959, had lingered around Swindon shed for a few months before making to the Works side for scrapping. Notice the missing front window glass and the incorrect power class 'C' within the yellow route availability disc, which should have been an 'A' (16,500-18,500lb tractive effort). *RCR 12901-13999 (325)*

Opposite bottom: Churchward Mogul No 6363 of Newton Abbot (83A) passes the Reception Shed with an up parcels van train, whilst classmate No 6331 and King No 6002 *King William IV* look on. The side of the Reception Shed facing the main running lines was enclosed with a substantial brick façade, whereas the steel frame on the remaining three sides was only partially clad in asbestos sheeting. Inside an overhead grab crane ran the full length of the building, the control cabin for which was accessed via the ladder and doorway seen in the end wall. The first two vehicles in the train are Collett K41/42 Gangwayed Passenger Brakes in carmine and cream livery with the third a Hawksworth K45/46 in plain carmine. 26 April 1959. *RCR 12901-13999 (331)*

Above: Dick has climbed on to one of the tenders seen to the right of the previous image in order to capture this unusual elevated view of County Class No 1002 *County of Berks*. It has just emerged from a Heavy Intermediate where it retained the boiler and double chimney fitted the previous June, but has received a full repaint. Once paired with tender No 104 and run in, it returned to Penzance (83G) shed on 3 May. This busy view also captures new build BR Standard 9F 2-10-0 No 92205, Modified Hall No 6960 *Raveningham Hall* and a parade of boilers waiting to be moved on the traverser into the Boiler Shop. 26 April 1959. *RCR 12901-13999 (332)*

Above: Standard Class 5 4-6-0 No 73017 approaches Swindon alongside the Conyard sidings with an Up passenger working from Westbury on 26 April 1959. Formerly a Western Region locomotive, it had been transferred from Swindon (82C) to Weymouth Radipole (71G) in October 1958 and the Southern influence can be seen with the converted forward facing lamp irons. The train is formed of a mixed collection of ex-GWR coaches and a FRUIT D van behind the tender. In the background Rushey Platt Junction diverges to the left towards Swindon Town Station and the bridge carrying the M&SWJR over the GW main line to Bristol can be seen in the distance. *RCR 12901-13999 (334)*

Opposite top: The six members of the Collett 1366 Class (1366-1371) were built as a modern pannier tank version of the short wheelbase outside cylinder 1361 Class saddle tanks. Constructed at Swindon in 1934, they were chiefly employed within the tightly curved Carriage and Wagon Shops and whilst most were redeployed, Nos 1371 and 1369 remained resident throughout the 1950s. Here the pair are stabled for the weekend on the kickback siding next to the Coal Stage on Sunday 6 September 1959. No 1369 was destined for preservation, after operating for its final few years on the freight only Wenford Bridge branch in Cornwall until November 1964. *RCR 14000-15099 (239)*

This page, bottom: One of Dick Riley's most frequently published colour photographs taken at Swindon shed is a portrait of ex-works Castle No 5049 *Earl of Plymouth* from 6 September 1959. This black and white version was captured from the opposite side earlier in the day, as the pristine Newton Abbot locomotive is prepared for its journey back to South Devon. This angle shows off to good effect the huge proportions of the newly fitted double chimney and also visible is the often-missed cab front window wiper. It was common practice at 82C for numbers to be chalked on engines, to indicate to drivers on to which road they were to be stabled. *RCR 14000-15099 (242)*

Churchward's imposing 47xx Class looked truly majestic in BR lined green, especially when as clean as No 4703 on 6 September 1959. Only nine of these 5' 8" wheeled 2-8-0s were built between 1919 and 1923, designed specifically for hauling seventy-wagon vacuum-fitted fast freights non-stop over long distances. This was one of the class to have its sniffing valves mounted outside the steam chest, resulting in them protruding through the cylinder casing, the standard position being on the smokebox saddle. Collett had proposed the fitting of his side window cab and naming the class after former broad-gauge goods engines, but this was rejected by the GWR Directors, which is a shame as *Behemoth*, *Dreadnought*, *Gladiator*, *Hercules* and *Mammoth* would have proved most suitable. *RCR 14000-15099 (262)*

Top: Dick first encountered 2-6-2T No 3100 during its construction in 1938 on page 16. Here it is again in storage between classmates No 3102 and 3101 on sidings to the side of the Stock Shed on 6 September 1959. By this time it had become common for withdrawn locomotives to be stored in and around the Stock Shed and Gasworks, partly due to the burgeoning numbers in the Conyard, but also as from March 1959 consignments were being sold to private scrap contractors and towed away for disposal. This trio were to linger until finally being cut up in February 1961. *RCR 14000-15099 (243)*

Bottom: 2301 Class 'Dean Goods' 0-6-0 No 2516 was another locomotive earmarked for preservation, and its movement around the Swindon Works site followed a similar pattern to that of No 4003 *Lode Star*. Arriving in May 1956 following withdrawal from Oswestry shed it spent a number of years in storage within, and as seen here alongside the Stock Shed. This March 1897 built locomotive was one of a class of 260 constructed at Swindon between 1883-1899, and was to be the penultimate one in revenue service. Both the locomotive and its Dean 2500g tender are the only examples to survive, as part of the National Collection and are today displayed at Swindon within STEAM – Museum of the Great Western Railway. 6 September 1959. *RCR 14000-15099 (245)*

Some 21 years and 4 months after Dick first photographed it fresh from build (page 10), Collett 2884 Class No 2890 has returned to its birthplace for a much needed Heavy General on 6 September 1959. Recently arrived from Banbury (84C) shed it shares the reception sidings alongside the General Offices with a mixed trio of tank engines and if you ever wondered what the inside of a running plate toolbox looks like, check out the 0-4-2T! The 2-8-0 is already devoid of its safety valve bonnet and part of the front handrail, but following overhaul it remained local with a transfer to 82C and would go on to provide sterling service until April 1965.

The original Works Main General Office block was built as a two-storey structure in 1843, later expanded with a new wing at right angles in the 1860s and with the top floor Drawing Offices added as a further extension in 1904. It was during this final building work that the pair of stone locomotive bas-reliefs were incorporated above the new entrance doors facing the Bristol main lines. RCR 14000-15099 (246)

Originally mounted at each end of the 1840 Broad Gauge Engine Shed that sat adjacent to the Bristol line, the pair of stone carvings depict a 2-2-2 locomotive and tender, which are purported to represent one of Brunel's early 7' 0¼" gauge purchases named *Premier*. When the shed was earmarked for demolition the reliefs were placed in safe storage, until assuming the position they retain to this day. *RCR 14000-15099 (250)*

Above: Heavily stripped Collett 5101 Class Large Prairie No 5160 on the arrivals sidings at 'The Pool' on 6 September 1959. It had been officially withdrawn from Hereford on 25 November 1958, but evidence suggests it then spent time as a stationary boiler (hence the chimney fitting) before making its way to Swindon for scrapping. Built as part of Lot. 259 in October 1930, it operated from Leamington Spa, Birkenhead, Stourbridge, Stafford Road and Chester in addition to Hereford, accumulating 679,992 miles in the process. Notice how the boiler of the 2-6-2T and that of 2-8-0T No 4217 behind, show the riveted oval patch above the smokebox saddle that indicate they were previously fitted to locomotives with outside steampipes. *RCR 14000-15099 (248)*

Opposite top: One can only wonder at the Health & Safety implications of being this close to running lines and moving trains today, but empowered with his Lineside Pass, Dick Riley was able to capture stunning images such as this. On 6 September 1959, No 7028 *Cadbury Castle* (87E) heads the (023) 8.30am Sundays Only Swansea-Paddington past 'The Pool'. The locomotive is adorned with the characteristic Landore white painted buffers, whilst its ten-coach train barely features two vehicles of the same type. The Engine History Card shows the Castle entering Swindon for a Heavy General overhaul on the Monday, so it will almost certainly be about to be removed from the train in Swindon Station. *RCR 14000-15099 (249)*

Opposite bottom: Whilst Swindon Works was not involved with the construction of the Riddles Standard Class 5 4-6-0s, with Derby and Doncaster doing the honours, as a number of them were allocated to the Western Region they were regular visitors for overhaul work. From November 1956 when Swindon began to widen the application of lined green livery to ex-GWR classes previously dictated to be black, it was not long before BR Standard locomotives allocated to BR(W) sheds were similarly treated. This is rumoured to have originated from the Shedmaster at Shrewsbury, who requested that his stud of Class 5s were painted green following shopping. Thus the application of 'Shrewsbury Green' became common practice, to also include WR Class 4 4-6-0s, Class 3 2-6-2Ts, Class 2 2-6-0s and whilst a special one off, most famously 9F 2-10-0 No 92220 *Evening Star*, the last steam locomotive constructed in the Works. It is proffered that the result did somewhat lift the austere lines of the Standards, as seen here on No 73054 next to the Iron Foundry on 6 September 1959. *RCR 14000-15099 (252)*

Old Oak Common's No 6009 King Charles II passes the Works hauling the (331) 11.15am SuO Paddington-Taunton via Bristol. The consist of the train very much typifies the mixture of coaches assembled for weekend and relief workings, but does notably include catering facilities. The presence of fresh ballast alongside the Down line suggests that relaying with flatbottom rail is imminent during an upcoming weekend engineering possession. Behind the signal post can be seen the chimneys of the Central Boiler Station, which numbered eight and were believed to be made up from the surplus boiler barrels from withdrawn Dean Goods locomotives, and if you look really closely the two Works Hooters can be discerned between the first pair of chimneys. 6 September 1959. *RCR 14000-15099 (256)*

Another Landore Castle hauled express sees No 4094 *Dynevor Castle* approaching Swindon with the (028) 6.45am SuO Fishguard Harbour-Paddington. The locomotive retains an original two row superheated boiler but has had its fluted 'Vauxhall' inside cylinder casing replaced by a later box-shaped version. On the left is the cavernous entrance to the six-road Newburn Carriage Shed, capable of stabling 265 bogie coaches and measuring some 1,800ft long by 122ft wide. The wagons to the right, including an N30 10-ton loco coal diagram of 1935, contain coal removed from locomotive tenders and bunkers within the Reception Shed prior to overhaul. 6 September 1959. *RCR 14000-15099 (258)*

Above: A venerable old locomotive in the shape of Churchward 45xx Class Small Prairie 2-6-2T No 4507 waits to be processed in the Reception Shed on 6 September 1959. Built at Wolverhampton Works in May 1907 as No 2168, it was part of the mass-renumbering programme of December 1912. By now the last surviving pre-WW1 stepped running plate early series 45xx, it had already gained lined green livery and surprisingly had not arrived at Swindon for scrapping but was to undergo a full overall and return to traffic. Destined to be the final Wolverhampton built locomotive in service, it was eventually withdrawn from Yeovil shed on 10 October 1963, before making its way to Bird's of Risca for scrapping in June 1964. *RCR 14000-15099 (257)*

Opposite: On 6 September 1959, 2884 Class No 3866 of Aberdare (86J) shed has just been released from 'A' Shop, having been 'heeled and soled' during an Intermediate overhaul. There is a wealth of interesting detail in this photograph; notice the crude boiler barrel patch repair on the 2-8-0, former private owner branding on the 9-plank wooden open wagon and newly fabricated tanks on the trolley destined for 2-8-2T No 7205. The D8xx Warship Class under construction inside the (AE) Erecting Shop is likely to be either No D811 *Daring* or No D812 *The Royal Naval Reserve 1859-1959*. *RCR 14000-15099 (260)*

Opposite: Broadside view of Castle Class No 4077 *Chepstow Castle* fresh from its final Heavy Intermediate, in front of the south elevation of the 'J' Shop Iron Foundry. This architecturally attractive stone built building was opened in 1873 and twice extended, for the final time in 1923 bringing it to a total size of 660ft by 80ft. From this angle it is easy to appreciate the neat elegant proportions of a single chimney Castle, with only a wayward open mudhole cover spoiling the perfection. Looking at this photograph it is hard to believe that today behind the regimented rows of windows a bright clinically clean retail emporium has replaced the filthy workshop, where once complex components for Great Western locomotives such as cylinder blocks were cast. 6 November 1960. *RCR 15100-16250 (370)*

Above: Here we see Dean Goods 0-6-0 No 2516 again, this time standing outside the Reception Shed on 6 November 1960. Quite why it had moved over to this side of the Works from the Stock Shed is uncertain, but it does appear to have temporarily been separated from its tender. The cosmetic restoration of the locomotive was to begin in earnest in October 1961 inside 'A' Shop, preparing it for display within the new Great Western Railway Museum in Faringdon Road across in the Swindon Railway Village. It was to be the first locomotive placed within the former Wesleyan Chapel on 9 April 1962 and was to be joined by replica broad gauge 2-2-2 *North Star*, Hawksworth 0-6-0PT No 9400, Churchward 4-4-0 No 3717 *City of Truro*, 4-6-0 No 4003 *Lode Star* and Diesel Railcar No 4. *RCR 15100-16250 (373)*

Above: The new order of Works Pilot is represented by 0-6-0DM Shunter No D2167 at the entrance to the Conyard on 6 November 1960. In traffic for less than a week, this was one of 148 examples built at Swindon from a class total of 230. Whilst nineteen similar locomotives were to be allocated to Swindon, this example was destined for the North Eastern Region and Darlington (51A) shed, and is captured here undergoing running trials. As previously seen, GWR shunting trucks were a standing feature coupled to 'Works Pilots' at Swindon, carrying both men and tools required for the duty; but these vehicles were soon to provide the secondary function of enabling a sufficiently long wheelbase able to activate section detection apparatus following the onset of colour light signalling. Fitted with a 204hp Gardner engine, these compact little shunters were to become Class 03 under the TOPS scheme, and following renumbering to 03167 in January 1973, this locomotive was withdrawn on 20 July 1975 and broken up at Doncaster Works. *RCR 15100-16250 (378)*

Opposite: Beautifully lit by the afternoon sun on 6 November 1960, Dick captured this broadside portrait of Collett 2-8-0 No 3824 waiting its turn on the weighbridge following overhaul. The cabin to the left provided accommodation for the Yardmaster and the Pilot Enginemen and Shunters that worked the Conyard and Sawmills Yards, reputedly also being the place to get the best mug of tea in the whole of Swindon Works! The 6-ton traversing crane to the rear serviced the (AW) Wheel Shop, the entrance doors to which are just out of shot to the right. *RCR 15100-16250 (376)*

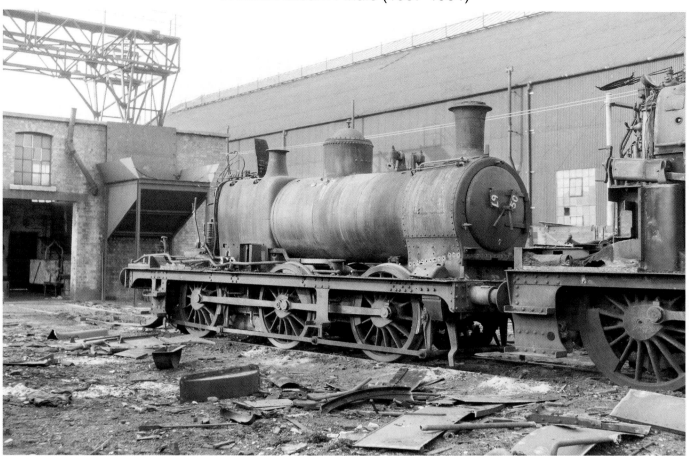

Opposite top: Slightly further along into the Conyard from the previous image, we find a lonely looking No 6801 *Aylburton Grange*, devoid of tender but otherwise totally complete. The first of the Grange Class to be removed from service, the locomotive spent the majority of its life working from Penzance shed and had the reputation of being a 'pet' favourite, possibly due to it being damaged but surviving the infamous Newton Abbot Blitz of 20 August 1940. As such it was usually kept impeccably presented and Dick noted that it had even received the attention of the Cornish shed's cleaners prior to its last journey to Swindon for withdrawal, although days of open storage had already masked the shine. The electric powered Goliath crane gantries surrounding the 'C' Shop dominate the skyline. 6 November 1960. *RCR 15100-16250(379)*

Opposite bottom: It is remarkable how frequently withdrawn locomotives were moved around the Conyard, as in the month preceding this photograph Dukedog No 9015 was marshalled next to a Collett Goods 0-6-0 and a 57xx 0-6-0PT. The date is now 6 November 1960 and it is in the company of 94xx Class 0-6-0PT No 9496 and 5101 Class 2-6-2T No 5150. The 4-4-0 had made its way to Swindon from Machynlleth in June and was to be broken up within a fortnight, whilst the Large Prairie, still reasonably clean in green with the Newton Abbot Works style of lining running beneath the cab side shutter and handrail, succumbed by the end of December. To the rear can be seen the north side Sawmill Stores and some of the huge quantities of cut timber stacked and awaiting transfer to other areas of the Works and elsewhere around the Western Region. *RCR 15100-16250 (384)*

Above: Collett 8750 0-6-0PT No 6750 nears the end of its existence as the scrapman completes his work. The first of the post-war batch of non-vacuum fitted panniers intended solely for shunting work, it entered service on 27 June 1947 fitted with a modern high cab and welded tanks, not that a trace of either still exists. Spending the majority of its life working from Barry shed, it did latterly move to Aberdare where it was utilised as a stationary boiler for its final year before despatch to Swindon for disposal. It is interesting to view the internal anatomy with the panniers removed and to see the top feed pipework and steam dome, usually obscured by the covers. 6 November 1960. *RCR 15100-16250 (385)*

Above: Prior to the preserved celebrity status that it enjoys today, Newton Abbot's No 7029 *Clun Castle* rests on shed following a weekend working up from the West Country. Looking uncharacteristically work stained for one of the Devon shed's top link locomotives, it also appears to have lost one of its inside valve spindle covers. Fitted with a double chimney in October 1959, the mechanical lubricator was repositioned forward of the steampipes at the same time. Surviving to the very end of steam on the Western Region, *Clun Castle* was sold in working order for its scrap value of £2,400 to Patrick Whitehouse in January 1966, to begin a fruitful second career working steam charters, a role it still performs from its base at Tyseley. 13 May 1961. *RCR 15100-16250 (646)*

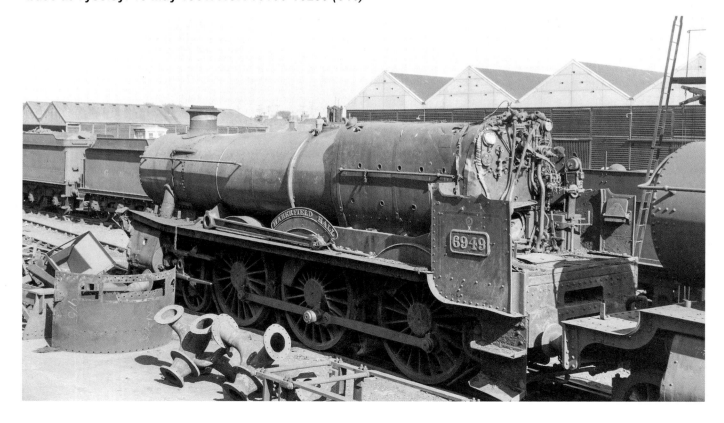

Opposite bottom: On 13 May 1961, Dick was to record the sad remains of No 6949 *Haberfield Hall*, which had been officially withdrawn following inspection the previous day. The Hall was at the head of the 6.37pm Wellington-Chester express on 13 February 1961, when travelling at around 45 mph it struck a freight train that was partially obstructing the main line at Baschurch, north of Shrewsbury. The locomotive and first two vehicles (a stores van and a corridor brake second) of the passenger train overturned, tragically killing the driver and fireman on the footplate and a worker in the leading van which caught fire. After recovery and initial storage at Shrewsbury shed, No 6949 was moved to Swindon for assessment, which concluded it was beyond economic repair. It was to be quickly despatched to 'C' Shop and had been cut up by 3 June. *RCR 15100-16250 (649)*

This page, top: An unusual viewing angle of Hawksworth County Class 4-6-0 No 1014 *County of Glamorgan* by the turntable on 13 May 1961, preparing to be lit following a Heavy Casual overhaul. The Reception Shed BSE staff

were responsible for slowly bringing the freshly shopped locomotives up to light steam, initially with off cuts of wood and oily rags in the grate, before being gradually supplemented with coal to bring up the boiler pressure. Once the attendant Boiler Inspector was satisfied all was well and the engine vacuum brake was tested, engines would be handed over to a Works Driver for transfer up to the Weighbridge House. All testing must have been satisfactory on this occasion as it returned to Bristol St Philips Marsh shed three days later. As a footnote to this image, whilst the original *County of Glamorgan* was scrapped in Cashmore's yard at Newport in December 1964, a replica utilising components from former Barry scrapyard residents is taking shape at the Great Western Society at Didcot. The decision to assume the identity of No 1014, is in recognition of the vital assistance given to the project by the Vale of Glamorgan Council and in homage to the legendary Dai Woodhams yard. *RCR 15100-16250 (651)*

This page, bottom: Churchward 47xx 2-8-0 No 4705 stands on the Water Sidings adjacent to Platform 8 on 13 May 1961, about to shunt its three coach formation into the Station to form a stopping service to Didcot, as a loaded test run. These five sidings were so named after a reservoir that once occupied the site and provided water for the Works and Station. This low angle shows off to good effect the large Standard No 7 boiler fitted exclusively to the class and the white X below the route availability disc signified the locomotive was permitted to haul loads heavier than officially specified for their power classification. It is thought that Dick Riley was able to enjoy a footplate trip on this return journey to Didcot, as he recorded the locomotive at various locations along the way. *RCR 15100-16250 (653)*

Above: The date is Sunday 24 June 1962 and an ex-works No 6874 *Haughton Grange* of Penzance (83G) shed sits paired with Collett 3500g tender No 2250, following its final Heavy General overhaul. It has been prepared by the BSE staff for running trials over the next few days, to conclude what was to be its last ever visit to Swindon Works. Note the addition of the Overhead Electric Warning flashes that had been introduced on to steam locomotives from around 1959 with the electrification of the Great Eastern Section. Swindon was slow in the application of this policy, no doubt due to the lack of 25kv wires on the Western Region. No 6874 was to be withdrawn and stored at Oxford shed on 10 September 1965, prior to being sold to Cashmore's at Great Bridge and scrapped during the December. Adjacent to the De-Tubing House can be seen a Castle Class boiler fitted with a double chimney and four row superheater, and an ex-works BR Standard Class 9F. *RCR 16610*

Opposite top: The 28xx and 2884 Class of 2-8-0s provided the mainstay of Great Western main line heavy freight power for over sixty years, earning them the deserved reputation as being one of the finest locomotives of their type in the country. Carrying the last style of BR black, No 3801 of Severn Tunnel Junction (86E) has emerged from an Intermediate overhaul where it has received a refurbished boiler and Churchward 3500g tender, which appears to be filled with the dreaded ovoids and coal dust. In addition to the obvious side window cab, this view clearly shows the whistle shield and modified shape of the upper motion bracket that were features of the later Collett examples. 24 June 1962. *RCR 16612*

Opposite bottom: No 6928 *Underley Hall* of Pontypool Road (86G), fresh from its final Heavy General, stands by the recently repainted doors of the Weighbridge House on 24 June 1962. Opened in 1906, the two-road building contained balancing pans and gauges for measuring the load weights being placed upon each driving wheel and the associated equipment to adjust the leaf springs to balance the locomotive. This structure survives today, tastefully restored and extended as a restaurant and micro-brewery. To the rear are the pitched gables of the (AW) Wheel Shop, which was completed in March 1920 and housed the 'A' Shop Offices in the closest wing. One of the new Western Class of diesel hydraulics in overall maroon livery can just be glimpsed, probably either D1005 *Western Venturer* or D1006 *Western Stalwart* that were completed that month. *RCR 16614*

Opposite top: On 24 June 1962 an impressive but macabre line of locomotives await their fate alongside 'A' Shop. Identifiable are Nos 5024 *Carew Castle*, 5006 *Tregenna Castle*, 4085 *Berkeley Castle*, 5090 *Neath Abbey*, a 43xx, a Hall, and No 4086 *Builth Castle*. An all too familiar scene by this date, as express passenger steam locomotives were being replaced by diesel hydraulics on Western Region top link services. As an ample stock of spare components now existed, the final act of Swindon Works would be to remove the name and numberplates for safekeeping and eventual sale disposal. All of the Castles in this photograph were to form part of a consignment purchased by John Cashmore Ltd and moved to their scrapyard at Newport for cutting. *RCR 16615*

Opposite bottom: A more uplifting sight is provided by a Southern Region interloper in the form of Maunsell LN Class No 30850 *Lord Nelson* arriving on the Home Counties Railway Club Special (Paddington - Swindon charter) on the same day, 24 June 1962. Built at Eastleigh Works in August 1926, the big 4-6-0 was in its final weeks of service before it too was withdrawn on 18 August, but to be preserved as part of the National Collection. It is certain that Dick Riley did not travel on the train, as he was at Exeter the previous day and had been photographing at Bath shed that morning. To the right is Rodbourne Lane Signal Box, which contained 31-levers and had been known simply as Swindon 'F' until 1909. This must have been a wonderful vantage point from where to observe the continuous activity alongside the Works. *RCR 16616*

Above: Having been turned on the Work's 65ft Ransomes & Rapier table, *Lord Nelson* is about to be coaled and watered in readiness for its return journey to Paddington. In addition to preparing locomotives for test runs following overhaul, the facilities at the Reception Shed were occasionally used to service visitors such as this, which would routinely use the Work's Engine Sidings to run round their train. 24 June 1962. *RCR 16619*

Above: An overall view of the front of the 1871 Locomotive Shed building showing all nine roads on 24 June 1962. Visible locomotives include a pair of 0-6-0DM Shunters (within the shed), an unidentified 2884 Class 2-8-0, classmate No 3832, Hall No 5978 *Bodinnick Hall* and Castle No 5075 *Wellington*. Although all facets of the steam shed were still operational at this date, an air of dilapidation was setting in as the onset of dieselisation was becoming increasingly prevalent. Many of the Pilot Link duties were now in the hands of diesel shunters and diesel-fuelling facilities had been installed on the sidings alongside No 9 Road, which is ironically where the tanks and hoses of the refuelling station for the post war oil burning experiment had been sited. *RCR 16620*

Opposite top: County Class No 1000 *County of Middlesex* leads a line of withdrawn locomotives stored adjacent to the Stock Shed, which is now housing Diesel Multiple Units. The pioneer of Hawksworth's most powerful 4-6-0 design had been withdrawn on 8 July 1964 after spending its last six months working from Swindon shed. It was sold for disposal to Cashmore's yard in Newport, where in excess of five hundred ex-GWR and BR(W) locomotives were to be scrapped.

To the right can be seen the remains of the Great Western Railway Gas Works that had closed in 1959 and was at one stage the largest private gasworks in the world. The elevated and inclined sidings allowed trainloads of wagons to deliver coal into the retort house and remove the coke briquettes left over after the gas had been extracted from the coal. As the relentless cull of steam continued, all of these available sidings and others around the Works became filled with locomotives awaiting their fate. 16 August 1964. *R17501 (198)*

Opposite bottom: A distinguished visitor in the shape of LNER Gresley A3 Class 4-6-2 No 4472 *Flying Scotsman* is serviced at Swindon shed during its layover whilst hauling the Warwickshire Railway Society 'Swindon & Eastleigh Tour' on 16 August 1964. The famous pacific had received a full overhaul at Doncaster Works and restoration to its late 1920s guise during early 1963, complete with refitted single chimney, corridor tender and LNER apple green livery. It then toured the country under the ownership of Alan Pegler, including numerous trips over Western Region metals, until departing to tour the United States in 1969. Behind the A3, the Coaling Stage is showing distinct signs of decay with little over two months of active usage remaining, although this angle shows the bricked up area of wall where once an additional coal tip featured on the southern elevation. *R17501 (199)*

Right: D95xx Class 0-6-0DH No D9505 stands gleaming in its fresh two-tone green paintwork on 16 August 1964. The new types of traction were now dominating the shed yard as dieselisation of the Western Region proliferated. The locomotive is one of fifty-six 650hp diesel hydraulic shunters built at Swindon and nicknamed 'Teddy Bears', purportedly following a quip by Works Foreman George Cole who lamented, 'We've built the Great Bear, now we're going to build a Teddy Bear'. Designed for yard shunting and local freight transfer

trips, the work for which they were intended was already on the decline due to an increasing preference for road transport. The class were to gain the distinction of being the last locomotives constructed at Swindon for use on the British Railways network. With the release of D9555 from 'A' Shop in October 1965, a lineage tracing back to April 1846 when Gooch's 2-2-2 *Great Western* became the first locomotive built entirely at Swindon, sadly came to a close. *R17501 (201)*

Bottom: One of the final photographs in the Dick Riley collection taken at Swindon is this view inside the deserted original straight shed on 16 August 1964, looking north towards the 45 ft turntable and archway through to the Smithy and Fitters' Workshop at the rear. It was routine for tank engines to be stabled around this turntable with one connecting road through the aperture to the right into the 1908 roundhouse extension shed. The straight No 5 Road is to the left of centre and it would appear some rudimentary coaling has been taking place within the building itself. The Shed was to officially close on 2 November 1964 with all remaining servicing conducted at Bristol and Reading, bringing to a close 93 years of housing steam locomotives on this site. *R17501 (202)*